I0803796

IMAGES
*of America*

# LAS VEGAS RADIO AND TELEVISION

After 50 years working in radio, I find there are many similarities to the theatrical performing arts in that people believe in superstition and curses. Like movie theaters that many claim are haunted, the particular mountain where this picture was taken, Mount Potosi, is "cursed." Just below the mountaintop, pieces of Carol Lombard's plane that crashed there remain to this day. This is a photograph I took of the remnants of the transmitter building for three radio stations after a fire in 1992 destroyed the contents of the building, leaving only the cinder block walls. After the structure was rebuilt, the roof caved in no less than three times due to heavy snow loads or falling ice from the tower that looms overhead. During winter, the only access was via helicopter until the FAA banned helicopters from the peak after a crash severely injured two engineers and the pilot. (Photograph by the author.)

**ON THE COVER:** Minister Elder Trent is pictured in the KTOO-AM 1280 studios on his radio show on Sunday, April 23, 1967. According to Federal Communications Commission (FCC) records, KTOO was first licensed by the FCC on April 27, 1956, as the second radio station licensed to the city of Henderson. It was the most powerful radio station in Southern Nevada, with 5,000 watts. The closest to it was KENO, which had 1,000 watts. However, KTOO was a "daytimer," which operated only during daylight hours, signing off every afternoon at sunset. (Courtesy of UNLV Library.)

IMAGES
*of America*

# LAS VEGAS RADIO AND TELEVISION

George Thomas Apfel
Foreword by Tom Hawley

ARCADIA
PUBLISHING

ISBN 978-1-4671-0644-3

Published by Arcadia Publishing
Charleston, South Carolina

Printed in the United States of America

Library of Congress Control Number: 2020950140

For all general information, please contact Arcadia Publishing:
Telephone 843-853-2070
Fax 843-853-0044
E-mail sales@arcadiapublishing.com
For customer service and orders:
Toll-Free 1-888-313-2665

Visit us on the Internet at www.arcadiapublishing.com

# Contents

# FOREWORD

As a teenager in Las Vegas, my goal was to become a showroom musician on the Strip, like my father. Later, in college, I discovered broadcasting. My years at KUNV 91.5 FM (the University of Nevada Las Vegas station) changed my direction. I've worked professionally in radio and, later, television since 1983 and have never looked back. For the past decade at KVBC (then KSNV, the Las Vegas NBC affiliate), I've increasingly focused on Southern Nevada history. George Thomas's *Las Vegas Radio and Television* ties these interests together. George was one of my earliest acquaintances in the world of broadcasting. I started professionally as a "board-op" and part-time DJ at KRAM 1340 AM. When the station added an FM counterpart, KITT 96.3, George—already a radio veteran by then—was one of the first hires, providing news updates on the combo. He switched to full-time DJ and engineering work, and I slipped into the news slot. It has been a wild ride ever since. Starting in the mid-1970s, George has been up and down the radio dial in Las Vegas both on the air and behind the scenes. While many of us have lived that life, George has chronicled and researched it along the way. He started sharing his work with a Facebook group and now reaches a wider audience with this book. In *Las Vegas Radio and Television*, we learn about the first radio station in this area, which is not the one usually getting the credit. We get the background on legendary local broadcasters like Hal Morelli, Red McIlvaine, and Walt Reno—names that still bring a smile to the faces of longtime Las Vegans—and an alphabet soup of K-stations, some of which have been popping up in different formats and dial positions for decades. The world of broadcasting is changing rapidly. To understand where we are going, we have to know where we come from. Read ahead to get a sense of the rich history of broadcasting in Southern Nevada. Then listen to some radio and watch some TV.

—Tom Hawley

# Acknowledgments

Great thanks go out to the person who helped jump-start my work on this book by sharing hundreds of images he had harvested for use in his news stories on KSNV News 3 and for writing the introduction for the book: Tom Hawley.

To Stacy Fott at the University of Nevada Las Vegas (UNLV) Special Collection, thanks for coming through in a short time in spite of the COVID-19 pandemic forcing reduced hours and staffing. Sarah J. Hulme of the Nevada State Museum faced the same issues. Both institutions had to shut down during the height of the pandemic, and both of you came through when I needed help. Thank you, Tom Willett, for sharing your pictures of KBMI in 1966 and 1967, when I listened to you as Herman Schmerdley, and from KLAV in 1978, in the studios I worked on moving.

In addition, thanks to Keith Stewart, longtime Las Vegas radio pro and friend, for sharing a look inside the 1970s KLUC Industrial Road studios. Len Howard, with whom I worked over 40 years ago, how I wish you were still with us; I had no idea about the hours you were on the radio every day, and your photographs are what Vegas radio of the 1950s and 1960s was all about. Thanks also go to David Gleason, who has assembled a terrific website that has been my bible of broadcasting: americanradiohistory.com.

Forty of my fifty years in radio broadcasting have been spent in Las Vegas; it is here where I learned my craft from the finest broadcasters in the business. On the programming end, thank you to great program directors (or PDs) such as Dave Anthony and Tim Maranville; production and voice talents like Sam O'Neil; and the engineers who became mentors, helping to satisfy my craving for technical knowledge: Jim Flint, Gordon Atteberry, Gordy Alsum, Joe Sands, and Tracy Teagarden. To all of my coworkers who became friends, you prove that the Las Vegas market has enjoyed great talent and true inspiration.

# Introduction

Las Vegas did not exist as a city, town, or village before the railroad established a stop along its new route, the first direct line between Salt Lake City and Los Angeles. Las Vegas is the only major western US city to be established in the 20th century. The railroad auctioned off lots around the new train depot in May 1905. The San Pedro, Los Angeles, & Salt Lake Railroad was not only responsible for creating the city, it was also the principal employer and provided water and power. John "J.M." Heaton, the railroad's supervisor for the new Las Vegas operation, became one of the city's elite citizens. He was the city's third weather observer, recording climate data from 1907 to 1909, according to NOAA and the National Weather Service Las Vegas.

It was the railroad that fueled Las Vegas's growth during the beginning of the 20th century, with gambling outlawed in the 1910s and 1920s. A national railroad strike hit the dusty desert town hard, but it eventually recovered. The city's location in the middle of the Mojave Desert may have been a factor in the many ranches that sprung up and featured prostitution and booze during Prohibition. The promise of a massive dam project and the construction of Boulder (now Hoover) Dam helped the town's population more than double between 1920 and 1930.

Just as Las Vegas did not form until 1905, the city was late to have its own radio station. In the early 1920s, nearby Los Angeles stations were able to be heard in Las Vegas. The 1927 annual report of the Federal Radio Commission to the Congress of the United States shows a construction permit issued to Heaton in Las Vegas for a 100-watt station at 1420 KHz. It would take two years for the station—KGIX—to first sign on. On September 12, 1929, the *Reno Gazette Journal* reported:

> The new Las Vegas broadcasting station will go on the air October 20, it was announced this morning by J.M. Heaton of the Las Vegas Broadcasting Company, which is now preparing for the installation of the station here. Heaton, aided by M.H. Marshall, general manager and part owner of KPLA and KMTR of Los Angeles, has been whipping the plant into shape during the past few days, and it is expected that the final announcement as to the location of the station be made soon. It was originally planned to put the station in one of the stores in the new building of P.J. Sullivan, but this has been altered, and it will be placed atop some local business house, Heaton announced. The station will be one thousand watt capacity, and will cost some $50,000 installed. Marshall will remain here for several days working out details of the prospect with Heaton, and it is expected that work on the station will be under way within the near future.

Ultimately, this station went dark for the final time around 1933. It would be seven more years before an engineer from Los Angeles decided to take a chance on this dusty desert town and establish what has become the oldest radio station in Las Vegas. Maxwell "Max" Kelch and his wife, Laura Belle, requested KLVN as their primary choice for call letters. According to a story in the February 7, 1999, *Las Vegas Review-Journal*, those calls were already taken, so the Federal Communications Commission (FCC) assigned the station their second choice: KENO. By the end of the decade, more stations came online with an interesting collection of call letters: KLAS and KRAM in 1948 and KORK in 1953. Las Vegas was unique in that the local strip resorts viewed having a radio station on their property as a status symbol; it made good economic sense to offer office and transmitter space in exchange for free advertising on trade. In 1953, every Las Vegas station had studios in Strip hotels or on hotel grounds.

The 1960s, 1970s, and 1980s saw explosive growth in the population of the metro area—a trend that culminated in the 1990s with the area becoming the fastest-growing metropolitan area according to US Census statistics. This dramatically changed the radio and television landscape, with many more stations signing on. Radio formats began to diversify, with the three basic formats—middle of the road (MOR), country, and Top 40—assuming new acronym assignments such as adult contemporary (AC), new adult contemporary (NAC), contemporary hit radio (CHR), and album-oriented rock (AOR). FM radio quickly evolved from being beautiful background music to the new format leader by the end of the 1970s. Las Vegas television grew from three network affiliates to one independent, then many more.

This book focuses on the beginnings of radio and television in Las Vegas and tells the story of an area that had no reliable local radio stations until 1940. While shifting from a market ranked at No. 173 in the United States in 1970 to No. 31 in 2020, Las Vegas has had an interesting ride getting close to the "Top 30."

# Las Vegas Radio and Television Stations

This list includes Las Vegas area radio and television stations in the order in which they signed on with their original call letters; the current call letters of the stations follow in parentheses.

**Radio**

- KGIX
- KENO
- KLAS (KLAV)
- KRAM (KKGK)
- KORK (KRLV)
- KBMI (KSHP)
- KTOO (KQLL)
- KRBO (KXST)
- KLUC-FM
- KVEG-AM (KNIH)
- KRGN-FM (KWID)
- KORK-FM (KXPT)
- KVEG-FM (KOMP)
- KLVM-FM (KMXB)
- KDWN
- KUDO-FM (KYMT)
- KMZQ-FM (KXQQ)
- KITT-FM (KKLZ)
- KLVV-FM (KXTE)
- KRLV (KSNE)
- KLSQ (KWNR)
- KMMK (KISF)
- KJUL (KFRH)

**Television**

- KLAS-TV 8
- KLRJ-TV 2 (KSNV-TV 3)
- KSHO-TV 13 (KTNV)
- KHBV-TV 5 (KVVU)

# *One*

# The Early Years

In 1927, seven years after Las Vegans first heard the magic of radio from stations in Los Angeles, local railroad agent J.M. Heaton applied for a construction permit for KGIX. The station was slated to begin around Christmas 1929 but had many difficulties, spending more time off the air than on. The *Union Pacific Magazine* reported in its August 15, 1931, issue that Heaton took a leave of absence from his job. Whether it was for health or personal reasons or to spend more time building a radio station is not known. *Broadcasting Magazine* reported in its October 15, 1931, issue that KGIX was granted permission to remain off-air until November 1 in order to finish work on the transmitter and to make tests. The Federal Radio Commission (FRC), the governmental regulatory body at the time, had recommended Heaton's license be canceled. The station continued to falter.

On January 27, 1932, Cannon Systems Ltd. applied for a construction permit for a new standard broadcast station at Glendale, California. At the time, Las Vegas was considered part of the Southern California region, and the FRC set station quotas for regions. In order to obtain approval and not exceed the region's quota, Cannon Systems requested that the facilities assigned to KGIX be withdrawn. The commission granted Cannon Systems' application, and in so doing, cut the time in half for KGIX's pending license renewal.

On February 16, 1933, the FRC tendered a construction permit for a new transmitter and studio location in the heart of downtown: the Palace Theater. The central location would help the 100-watt signal to be heard inside the city limits.

The following year, the Federal Radio Commission became the Federal Communications Commission (FCC). Heaton was unable to complete the construction of KGIX before the station's permit expired. On May 14, 1935, the FCC performed its first license deletion for KGIX. Only two weeks later, on June 1, 1935, Caroline Heaton, wife of J.M., applied for a construction permit for the 1420 KHz spot on the dial where KGIX had once existed. Just over a year later, the Glendale, California, group that challenged J.M. Heaton three years earlier filed for a construction permit for 1370 KHz.

Both stations apparently failed, and it would take five years before another station would launch in Las Vegas. In the meantime, residents tuned to the powerful Los Angeles radio stations, and an engineer at one of those stations relocated to Las Vegas with his wife to launch the first permanent radio station; he would also become a major factor in the growth of Las Vegas.

In their 2000 book *The First 100*, A.D. Hopkins and K.J. Evans write that in 1905, wealthy senator William A. Clark established a maintenance shop for his San Pedro, Los Angeles, & Salt Lake Railroad (now the Union Pacific). Clark purchased 110 acres and subdivided them into 1,200 lots. The lots were auctioned off, and since the area lacked permanent structures, a passenger car on a siding served as the first depot. (Courtesy of UNLV Library.)

Even though the city was in the middle of the Mojave Desert, there was an ample water supply from artesian wells, which flowed into geysers when drilled. In this May 10, 1924, photograph, three men identified as Mr. Wright (left), J.M. Heaton (center), and Walter Bracken observe a new well. Heaton managed the train depot and founded the city's first radio station in 1928. (Courtesy of UNLV Library.)

*Las Vegas Age* editor and publisher Charles "Pop" Squires dutifully took daily weather observations from a weather station supplied by the National Weather Service (NWS). The first observations were taken in the 1890s from the Kiel Ranch but are deemed unreliable. The first accurate records were taken by KGIX founder J.M. Heaton in 1909. According to NWS Las Vegas history, in 1911, Squires began daily observations outside his newspaper's downtown office. He was the first official Cooperative Observer Program participant recognized by the weather service in Las Vegas. He also was fascinated by the new technology called radio and often wrote about it in his paper. He became a frequent guest on KGIX and, later, KENO. (Courtesy of the National Weather Service Las Vegas.)

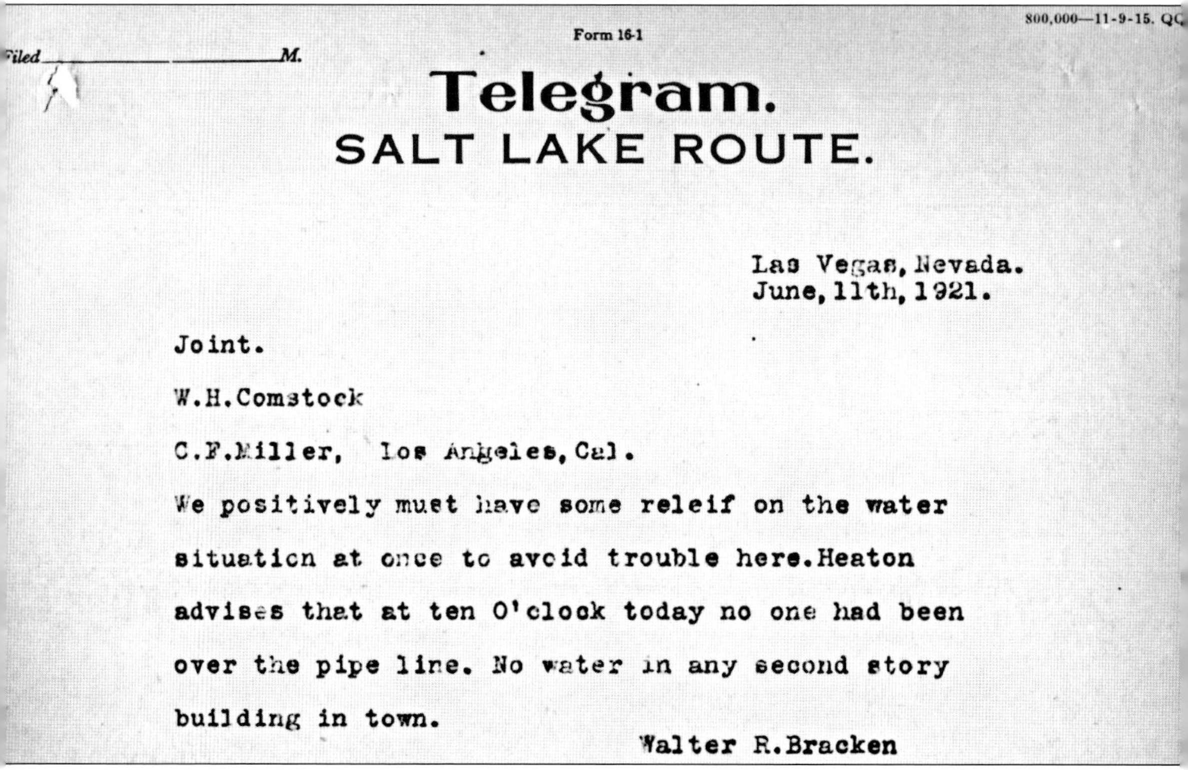

800,000—11-9-15. QC

Form 16-1

Filed ____________ M.

Telegram.

SALT LAKE ROUTE.

Las Vegas, Nevada.
June, 11th, 1921.

Joint.

W.H.Comstock

C.F.Miller, Los Angeles, Cal.

We positively must have some releif on the water situation at once to avoid trouble here.Heaton advises that at ten O'clock today no one had been over the pipe line. No water in any second story building in town.

Walter R.Bracken

As Las Vegas station agent, J.M. Heaton was in charge of the terminal and was the go-between for the railroad and town residents. The railroad not only provided electricity through one of their generators, it also built and maintained the city's water system that was in constant need of attention, according to numerous telegrams on the subject. (Courtesy of UNLV Library.)

age Eight Sunday, November 23, 19

# )bservations

## ADIO STATIONS

Las Vegas managed to get along without any radio sta on whatever for the first twenty-five years of its existence as wn. In fact when Las Vegas town lots were auctioned in 1905 uch a thing as a radio station through hich a person could reach out into in air and bring in the sound of usic or the voices of people, was un- nown. In fact it was along about 1920 hen a few people began to have re- eiving sets and tried, often wtih very oor success, to get music from the powerful," new, one-thousand watt ation established by The Los An- eles Times in Los Angeles.

Ernie Cragin and Bill Pike were e leaders in attempted radio recep- on in Las Vegas and bought in 1922 really up-to-the-minute receiving set r use in their Majestic Theater, lo- ated where the Golden Nugget now

C. P. Squires

Pictured is one of C.P. Squires's daily columns, which appeared on the front page of his newspaper *Las Vegas Age*. Las Vegas had its first exposure to the radio when Ernie Cragin and Bill Pike placed a "really up to the minute" receiving set on the stage at their Majestic Theatre. Cragin's name would appear in the call sign of the first FM stereo station in the state, KRGN-FM 101.9, in 1963. (Courtesy of UNLV Library.)

# Choose Site For Radio Station

## New Building On State St., To House Broadcasting Project to Start at Once.

Lot 1, block 1, on State street near Linden, in the Grand View tract of which Brydn & Neiswender, Los Angeles, are owners, has been chosen as the site of the new broadcasting station KGIX, it was announced yesterday.

Plans for the building to house the activity of the broadcasting company sponsored by J. M. Heaton and N. H. Marshall, have been prepared by James A. Fleming, architect in the Professional building.

The structure will be two stories in height and the first story will be devoted to the business of the company, the second subdivided into six apartments.

The lower floor will contain the music director's room; room for the public, from which through a 5x10 foot plate glass window they may view the performers; operator's room; dynamo room; broadcasting room and studio.

The building will be of frame construction. The towers which, it is understood, will be approximately 150 feet in height, will be built on the same lot.

This is an October 1, 1929, *Las Vegas Age* story about the selection of a site for KGIX. Las Vegas was a city of only 5,000 people, and the location was described as "way out in the country." The "dynamo room" contained the electric generator that supplied direct current for the transmitter and equipment. It is interesting that apartments were planned for the second floor. (Courtesy of UNLV Library.)

On February 16, 1933, the *Federal Register* showed a construction permit for a new 100-watt transmitter amended to request a change of transmitter and studio locality to the Palace Theatre building. (Courtesy of *Broadcasting Magazine*.)

## FEBRUARY 16

WLEY, Lexington, Mass.—Voluntary assignment of license to Albert S. Moffat.

KFAC, Los Angeles—Voluntary assignment of license to Los Angeles Broadcasting Co., Inc.

KFVD, Los Angeles—Voluntary assignment of license to Los Angeles Broadcasting Co., Inc.

KGIX, Las Vegas, Nev.—CP for new 100 w. transmitter amended to request change of transmitter and studio locally to Palace Theatre Bldg. and make changes in equipment.

Las Vegas's first radio station, KGIX, launched in 1929. Pictured is the transmitter building, which was then located at a spot considered to be "way out of town," as described in the *Las Vegas Age*. The building was located on N. Eighth Street just north of the expressway. As opposed to modern radio stations, which use vertical towers to transmit their signals, the KGIX station used what is called a "T-Top" antenna consisting of horizontal wires strung between two towers; the western tower is shown here on top of the building. (Courtesy of UNLV Library.)

## KGIX To Be On Air Again Soon, Said

Radio station KGIX, "The Voice of Boulder Dam" at Las Vegas, will be on the air again shortly, it was announced this morning by J. M. Heaton, owner, after receipt of word from Washington that he had been victorious in retaining his permit.

An examiner sent out by the raido commission recommended that the license be cancelled, but he was overruled and Heaton was given permission to change the location of his station and gain a renewal of his license.

Heaton convinced the commission he was in a position to re-establish service and that Las Vegas is in need of the broadcasting services of his station.

Plans call for establishing the station in the Palace Theatre building, Heaton says, and it would be open within a comparatively short time.

With KGIX branded as the "Voice of Boulder Dam," on June 23, 1933, the *Las Vegas Age* carried a story proclaiming that the on-and-mostly-off-again radio station was bound to be on the air again soon. While Boulder Dam raced toward completion ahead of schedule, the Depression and constant equipment failures led to many periods of KGIX being off the air. This technology was still in its infancy, and the troublesome child did not have many who could keep the complex equipment running. There is no doubt that the intense summer heat also complicated matters. (Courtesy of UNLV Library.).

Pictured is a March 19, 1932, *Las Vegas Age* advertisement for a live radio broadcast on KGIX from Lorenzi's Lake Park Dance Pavilion, featuring Al Johnson and his Six Green Jackets direct from Los Angeles. In the 1920s, 1930s, and 1940s, a good portion of radio programming came from live concert events, unlike the platter-spinning of DJs in the 1950s and beyond. (Courtesy of UNLV Library.).

Downtown's Majestic Theatre was one of two locations under consideration as the home of the broadcast studios, as the transmitter building was not equipped to handle live musical acts and was "way out of town." Plans were made (see page 17), but the station failed to remain on the air long enough to occupy the theater. (Courtesy of UNLV Library.).

Pictured here in Denver, Colorado, in January 1900 are, from left to right, Emma Marie "Peggy" (Schaefle) and William Norton Schuyler with John (J.M.) and Caroline Heaton. In addition to J.M. being the station agent for the San Pedro, Los Angeles, & Salt Lake Railroad in Las Vegas, he and Caroline were very successful in real estate in the Las Vegas Valley. Although their radio

venture failed after a relatively short time, they both amassed quite a bit of acreage in the valley, including large amounts of land south of town, which then contained prime farming and livestock areas. (Courtesy of UNLV Library.)

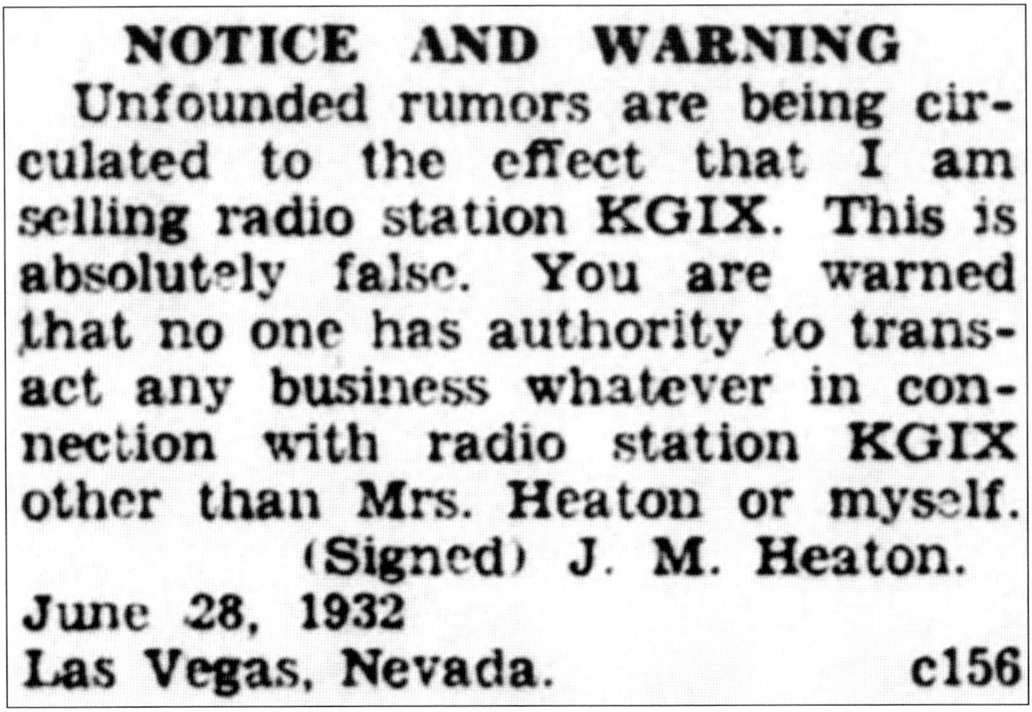

NOTICE AND WARNING

Unfounded rumors are being circulated to the effect that I am selling radio station KGIX. This is absolutely false. You are warned that no one has authority to transact any business whatever in connection with radio station KGIX other than Mrs. Heaton or myself.

(Signed) J. M. Heaton.

June 28, 1932

Las Vegas, Nevada. c156

The June 28, 1932, issue of the *Las Vegas Age* newspaper addressed rumors that the station was for sale. During this period (and for most of its brief history), the station struggled to stay afloat. Even with the boom from the construction of Boulder Dam, the combination of the Great Depression and equipment problems from operating in the intense heat of Las Vegas made life difficult for KGIX. On February 16, 1933, the Federal Radio Commission (FRC) issued a construction permit (CP) for "a new 100 w. transmitter amended to request change of transmitter and studio locality to Palace Theatre Bldg. and make changes in equipment." (See page 16.) Extensions for the CP were granted until the CP finally expired on May 14, 1935, and the license became the very first one to be deleted by the newly formed Federal Communication Commission. (Courtesy of UNLV Library.)

Pictured at left is Jack Heaton, station agent for what would become the Union Pacific depot in Las Vegas. Based on accounts in the *Las Vegas Age* as well as Federal Radio Commission documents, it appears Jack's wife, Caroline, had control of the family finances, as a 1935 attempt to revive the station came in papers filed by her. (Courtesy of UNLV Library.)

# *Two*

# THE WAR YEARS

After KGIX faded into the darkness in the mid-1930s, Las Vegas's only source for radio was from the higher-power stations in Southern California, like 50,000-watt KFI at 640 or KNX at 1050. Ham radio operator Max Kelch, who had a master's degree in physics from the California Institute of Technology, was on the engineering staff of the Warner Brothers station KFWB-950. Kelch first considered a career in teaching, but the money was poor, and the rapidly growing radio business was in need of technicians to keep stations on the air.

K.J. Evans chronicled Kelch's story in the *Las Vegas Review-Journal* on February 7, 1999:

> Kelch worked as a design engineer for Warner Brothers and was technical supervisor for such network programs as *Amos and Andy*. For Decca, he served as a recording engineer for artists such as Bing Crosby and Francis Langford. Laura Belle Gang was a native of Cincinnati who had lived in New York before coming to Los Angeles. In the late 1930s, she met Kelch at KFWB. "I was doing dramatic parts for an acting group," she said. In 1939, when Kelch took the job of chief engineer at station KGDM in the Sacramento Valley city of Stockton, Laura Belle went with him. That same year, they crossed the Sierra to Carson City and were married. They had already decided they wanted their own radio station by the time they were married. Kelch just needed to find the most promising spot to locate. "We did a survey of the Southwest, because that's where we wanted to live," said Laura Belle Kelch. That research revealed Las Vegas once had a radio station, KGIX, but it had gone off the air. No competition. Further inquiries revealed that the local business community would support a new radio station. "I thought it was wonderful," said Laura Belle Kelch, who was able to ride her horse downtown on errands. "I had never been in, or lived in a small town before." Of course, Las Vegas lacked the cultural amenities of larger cities, and Laura Belle soon found herself up to her elbows in civic and service activities. She was active in improving the Las Vegas Library and, as an accomplished watercolorist, was a founding member of the Las Vegas Art League. Charles "Pop" Squires took the mike occasionally to recall some slice of local history, or to hold forth on his own brand of rock-ribbed Republicanism. Kelch even offered the *Las Vegas Evening Review-Journal* a slot to pass along the day's headlines.

In November 1948, Max Kelch opened a new KENO radio facility on a plot of land on the south end of the El Rancho Vegas property. This was not only a huge increase in size and comfort (the original studios were next to the horse stables in the rear of the hotel), but it also featured an increase in power with a directional nighttime signal increasing from 250 to 1,000 watts and a

change in dial position from 1400 to 1460. Along with moving to new studios and a new place on the AM dial, KENO launched an FM station at 103.9—the first in the state and among the first in the country licensed after a World War II freeze. (Courtesy of UNLV Library.)

In the February 7, 1999, edition of the *Las Vegas Review-Journal*, Laura Belle Kelch recalled an offer made to her husband, Max, by El Rancho Vegas hotel owner Tommy Hull: "Max, if I moved your radio station, your tower, everything, to my property, would you move over there?" It was free studio space in a high-visibility location. Hull got a good deal, too—every 20 minutes or so, the announcer would identify the radio station and note that it was "broadcasting from the grounds of the fabulous El Rancho Vegas." (Courtesy of UNLV Library.)

KENO went on air in the fall of 1940 as an ABC affiliate serving a population of only 8,700. "Included in the entertainment," reported the *Las Vegas Evening Review-Journal*, "will be . . . 'Our Scenic Southwest,' devoted to promoting tourist interest in Southern Nevada and adjacent areas." KENO's first broadcast facility was the old Meadows Club building, constructed in 1931 by gambler Tony Cornero on Boulder Highway and Charleston Boulevard. The building itself was without heat in winter or cooling in summer and was literally falling down. (Courtesy of UNLV Library.)

The sign at right says, "Meadows Limited Whoopee," which befits the expressions on the faces of the club employees standing in front of the burned-out remains of the hotel. According to the *San Bernardino Sun*, because the hotel was located outside the Las Vegas city limits, the Las Vegas city fire department refused to fight the fire. In an oral history for the *Las Vegas Review-Journal*, Laura Belle Kelch dubbed it "the extinct nightclub" (Courtesy of UNLV Library.)

In 1945, the Live Wire Fund came to fruition with Max Kelch at its helm. The Live Wire Fund created a major push after World War II to bring tourism and hospitality to Las Vegas and played a major role in establishing legitimate gaming and hospitality as the city's main industry. Pop Squires wrote in the *Las Vegas Age*: "All businessmen should join in the campaign to spread the fame of Las Vegas to every part of the country in preparation for the vast surge of travel which the end of the war will start." With the Live Wire funds, the Las Vegas Chamber of Commerce hired the Walter Thompson Agency and, later, the West-Marquis firm in 1947. The firm created the first image of Vegas Vic with his tagline, "Howdy Podner." The artwork was later transformed into the iconic neon sign that is still on Fremont Street today. Kelch designed the audio system that boomed "Howdy Podner" to the public. (Courtesy of UNLV Library.)

**KENO was sold by Nevada Broadcasting Co. for $80,000 to newly formed company Nevada Broadcasting Co. Nevada Broadcasting is composed of E. Oncken (37.5%) news editor of KENO and managing editor of *Las Vegas Sun;* Ralph O. Dow (25%), chief engineer at KENO, and Merl Sage (37.5%), commercial manager at KENO.**

On April 3, 1955, the *Federal Register* reported the sale of KENO to three key employees of the station. Bid Weil was able to provide some specifics, as he worked there at the time (after starting in 1948): "Max offered the station for sale to his employees of whom I was one. Price: $87,000, with 5K down from each of us. Merle [*sic*] Sage the then manager came up with his as did some of the others. I could not make the cut. They then sold it to a group headed by a man name Sherwood from KING in Seattle. They moved the station to Flamingo just east of the Strip July 1, 1961." (Courtesy of *Broadcasting Magazine*.)

In this photograph dated March 9, 1956, the KENO radio remote vehicle is shown at the world premiere of *Meet Me in Las Vegas* in front of the El Portal Theatre on Fremont Street downtown. By the 1960s, the station—with its "hip" format and image—used a Volkswagen Microbus with "Color Channel 146" on the sides. In the 1970s, the station used the program director's custom-painted van, called the "KENO Shadow," to cruise the city streets, calling out license plates on cars with KENO bumper stickers in order to give out prizes. (Courtesy of UNLV Library.)

One of the most colorful and unique characters in Las Vegas radio was Jerry Roy, KENO general manager in the 1970s. Here, Roy (right) interviews Les Paul (left) and Mary Ford. I worked for Jerry Roy in the late 1970s at KENO-FM, and he had boundless energy as well as an incredible Mickey Mouse collection in his office. (Courtesy of Derek E. Roy.)

KENO general manager Jerry Roy is shown behind the KNBC microphone at Harrah's in Reno. During Roy's time running KENO, the company purchased an FM companion to the AM, KTRI-92.3 FM. As K-92 KENO-FM, it became the first AOR station in Las Vegas soon after it was purchased in mid-1977—a move intended to build an audience to help stave off a threat from rival KLUC-FM. The ratings performed well, but the station soon faced competition from another new AOR station: KFM-102. (Courtesy of Derek E. Roy.)

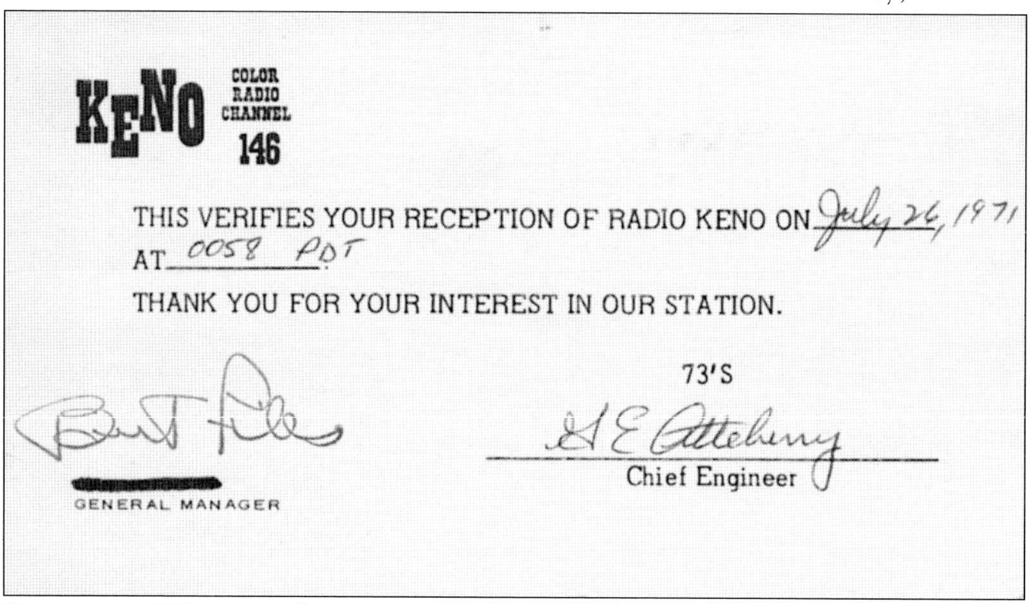
KENO COLOR RADIO CHANNEL 146

THIS VERIFIES YOUR RECEPTION OF RADIO KENO ON July 26, 1971
AT 0058 PDT

THANK YOU FOR YOUR INTEREST IN OUR STATION.

73'S

Burt Files
GENERAL MANAGER

G E Atteberry
Chief Engineer

Pictured is a QSL card verifying reception of radio KENO on July 24, 1971, signed by general manager (GM) Burt Files and Gordon E. Atteberry. Atteberry and I exchanged emails a few years ago, as we worked together at KLAV. He aspired to be a TV weatherman and was a talented magician and hypnotist as well as an incredible engineer. The owner of the radio station, Arthur Powell Williams (who also owned KSHO-TV at the time), told him to focus on engineering, where the best money was. Atteberry was an inspiration for me to go into engineering and taught me many aspects of the field during the time that we worked together. (Courtesy of Derek E. Roy.)

# *Three*

# The Fabulous 1950s

KLAS radio launched on March 1, 1948. The dusty desert town of Las Vegas only had only one radio station until then, and KLAS reused a transmitter location for KENO on the Meadows Club grounds, as the tower base and guy-wire anchors remained from KENO after that station left for the El Rancho.

Like KENO, KLAS radio set up shop in a hotel—downtown's Hotel Elwell. In the late 1940s, there was a two-lane highway to Los Angeles, US Highway 91, around which the center of the Las Vegas universe was moving. The El Rancho hosted KENO radio, and to the south, the Last Frontier was an up-and-coming resort on the Strip. In 1947, the Last Frontier was making plans for its Western Village, which would include state-of-the-art studios and offices for the newcomer in Las Vegas radio, KLAS, which had not yet signed on.

The FCC history cards for KLAS (KLAV) reveal a request submitted for its first studio location to change from the transmitter site at Thirtieth Street and Charleston Boulevard to the grounds of the Last Frontier in 1947; however, the application was canceled on request of the station's attorney on December 8, 1947. Instead, on March 8, 1948, the FCC approved the studio location request for Hotel Elwell, which would be the home of KLAS for just under two years. In January 1950, an application for KLAS to change studios to the Desert Inn Hotel was approved by the FCC.

Just weeks after KLAS signed on, KRAM became Las Vegas's third radio station. Also initially with studios in a downtown hotel, KRAM was slated to occupy the Desert Inn. Before the hotel was completed, KRAM used a standalone building in front of the hotel. *Las Vegas Age* publisher Pop Squires was excited about the new radio venture, and in 1948, he wrote in his column about newspaper publisher Hank Greenspun starting KRAM radio in the Desert Inn, where it remained for just over a year; KRAM then moved to the Flamingo, and KLAS moved into the completed Desert Inn. Ed Janson and Truman Hinkle were co-owners of KRAM when they signed the contract for the studios in the Flamingo. KRAM signed on at 920 on the dial; in the 1980s, they exchanged licenses with KORK to move to 1340.

In this photograph from April 1951, Wilbur Clark (in the dark suit, next to the microphone), listens to two female singers performing for CBS radio over KLAS-AM on the occasion of the first anniversary of Clark's Desert Inn. The singers are performing "I've Got a Date With Wilbur," which was written by Ted Mossman for the occasion. (Courtesy of UNLV Library.)

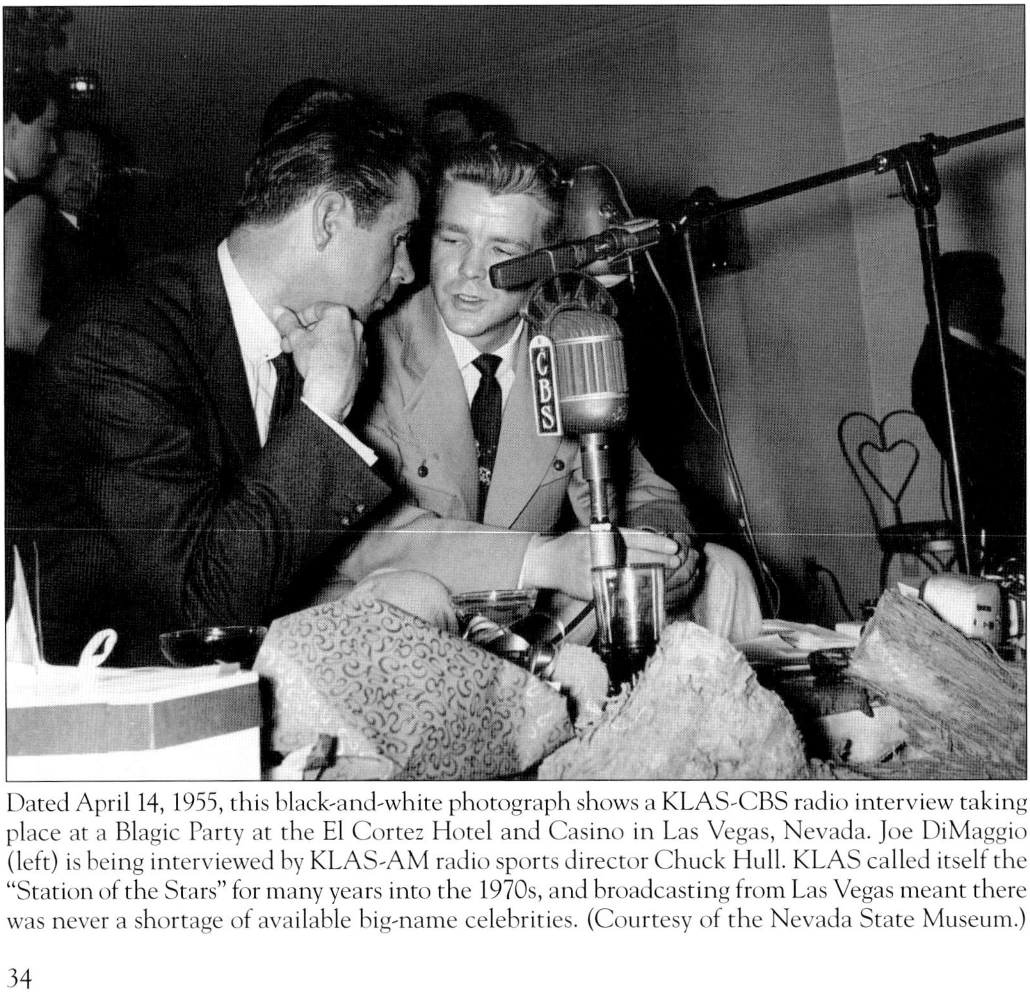


Dated April 14, 1955, this black-and-white photograph shows a KLAS-CBS radio interview taking place at a Blagic Party at the El Cortez Hotel and Casino in Las Vegas, Nevada. Joe DiMaggio (left) is being interviewed by KLAS-AM radio sports director Chuck Hull. KLAS called itself the "Station of the Stars" for many years into the 1970s, and broadcasting from Las Vegas meant there was never a shortage of available big-name celebrities. (Courtesy of the Nevada State Museum.)

This October 15, 1951, *Broadcasting Magazine* article is about the arrival of Las Vegas's fourth radio station, KORK. Very little is known of the early days of KORK due to the fact that the "history cards" for the station (in the FCC's old database) are not accessible. David McKay was president of the ownership group that included the stations listed in Reno and in Vallejo, California. (Courtesy of *Broadcasting Magazine*.)

# NEW NEVADA AM

## KORK to Take Air With NBC

KORK Las Vegas, Nev., announced last week that it was scheduled to go into regular operation "within a few days." KORK is the new NBC affiliate in Las Vegas, replacing KRAM. The new station will operate on 1340 kc with 250 w fulltime.

KORK is located on the grounds of the Hotel Thunderbird. David McKay, president of the new station, is also president of KOLO Reno and KGYW Vallejo, Calif. Manager Jack Kehoe is former sales manager of KOLO. Chief Engineer is Bill Binford.

This is an early-1950s photograph of the KORK studios, located to the rear of the Thunderbird Hotel on the Strip. The station's broadcast tower was behind the building. Vegas Valley Broadcast Group sold to Don Reynolds, who was granted the license in April 1955. Reynolds also owned KLRJ-TV2 and changed the call letters of his TV station to match the radio station on March 19, 1962. (Courtesy of UNLV Library.)

Pictured is an advertisement for the *Joe Julian Show* on KRAM. His legal name was Joseph Marandola; he operated a number of bars and liquor stores in Las Vegas. In 1956, he launched Southern Nevada's seventh radio station, a daytime-only AM at 1050 KRBO (for "Rainbow Broadcasting"). As was the case with all the other Las Vegas radio stations, it transmitted from the rear of the Last Frontier hotel. Marandola sold the property to Meyer "Mike" Gold in 1962. Gold changed the calls to KLUC and added an FM at 98.5, which was licensed for 24-hour operation. (Courtesy of Tom Hawley.)

Pictured are Freddie "The Champ" Baccari (left) of The Characters, a Vegas lounge act, and Len Howard on Howard's KRAM show, most likely at the Flamingo, where the studios were housed. (Although it may have been the Sahara, where Baccari performed in the lounge.) Howard was incredibly talented in many facets of radio and a true workaholic. He had multiple shows on two radio stations at different times on KLAS-AM and KRAM, and he also helped with UNLV football broadcasts in the 1980s. (Courtesy of Len Howard.)

"Mister Warmth" Don Rickles (left) is shown here as Len Howard's guest. In person, I found Rickles to be a considerate and respectful person, much unlike his stage persona. KRAM was actually the first station to play current popular hits that appealed to the teenage audience in the 1950s, according to a friend who would hang out with the nighttime DJ at the transmitter. The station's license required an operator to be on duty during nighttime hours, so the on-air person would load a tape at the studios, then at the Tropicana, which allowed him to make the trip to the transmitter on Twenty-Fifth Street and Owens Avenue to finish his shift. (Courtesy of Len Howard.)

Pictured here with Len Howard (center) are possibly Xavier Cougat (left) and an unidentified guest on Howard's KRAM 920 AM radio show. In early 1969, KRAM exchanged licenses with KORK to move from 920 to 1340, and KORK moved from 1340 to 920. There may have been a financial reason involved in the change, because the 1340 signal required only a single tower (so much less real estate would be involved). (Courtesy of Len Howard.)

This picture was taken in front of the KLAS radio microphone at the Blagic Party on April 14, 1955, at the El Cortez Hotel and Casino on Fremont Street in downtown Las Vegas. While the people are not identified, they possibly could be Fibber McGee and Molly being interviewed by a member of the KLAS staff. It was common to have major stars in front of radio microphones in Las Vegas. (Courtesy of the Nevada State Museum.)

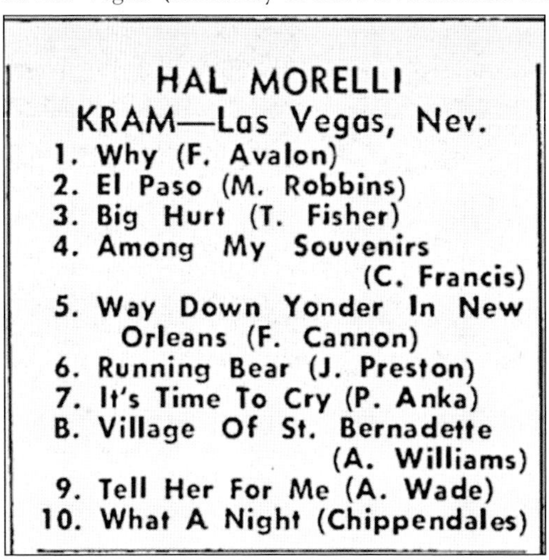

**HAL MORELLI**

**KRAM—Las Vegas, Nev.**

1. Why (F. Avalon)
2. El Paso (M. Robbins)
3. Big Hurt (T. Fisher)
4. Among My Souvenirs (C. Francis)
5. Way Down Yonder In New Orleans (F. Cannon)
6. Running Bear (J. Preston)
7. It's Time To Cry (P. Anka)
B. Village Of St. Bernadette (A. Williams)
9. Tell Her For Me (A. Wade)
10. What A Night (Chippendales)

In 1960, KRAM was the Top 40 station in Las Vegas—the one that most high school students listened to. A glance at this playlist from the February 23, 1960, issue of *Cashbox Magazine* backs up this point. For a brief time, KLAS-1230 AM enjoyed success playing the hits as "King Klas." That ended after the "Father of Automation," Paul Schafer, bought KLAS in 1961 to demonstrate how efficiently an automated station could run without people. The station ended up filing for bankruptcy and went into receivership in 1963. (Courtesy of *Cashbox Magazine*.)

The most popular radio (and later television) personality of the 1960s and 1970s was Red McIlvaine. He made the jump from KORK radio to KORK TV and became a regular fixture as a host on *Today at Noon* with Fred Willis. He voiced the identifications for the TV station with a unique style. He came from Los Angeles to work in Las Vegas, enjoyed success there, and briefly returned to Southern California before coming back to Vegas. (Courtesy of UNLV Library.)

"McIlvaine's Weathervane" was a regular sponsored feature on Red McIlvaine's morning radio show on KORK radio. He also acted as a TV weatherman on sister station KORK-TV 3. Another prominent local radio and TV personality who presented a daily dose of weather reports was McIlvaine's coworker Walt Reno. Unlike areas of the country that have to deal with hurricanes, tornadoes, and lake-effect snow, the only constant in Las Vegas weather is heat—although the monsoon season can deliver unpredictable results. (Courtesy of Tom Hawley.)

Walt Reno joined the staff of KORK radio in 1972 as an afternoon drive host. He later became the weatherman for KORK-TV. He did all kinds of radio and television commercials and quickly became the most recognizable broadcaster in Las Vegas in the 1970s and 1980s. When he made the move from KORK to KVEG radio, a country station, in the early 1980s, his ratings soared, and he became the No. 1 morning host in Las Vegas. Reno (left) is pictured on the golf course with Arnold Palmer. (Courtesy of Jamie Reno.)

# *Four*

# In Henderson, of Course

Southern Nevada got much more populous in the postwar years amid the success of promoting tourism and gaming. After World War II, it became home to two more stations, both of which signed on in the mid-1950s and were licensed in Henderson, Las Vegas's neighbor to the southeast: KBMI-AM 1400, first licensed on April 15, 1954, and KTOO-AM 970, first licensed on May 18, 1956. The "BMI" stood for the principal manufacturing plant in Henderson, Basic Magnesium, Inc., which had been a major player in the war effort for both World War II and Korea.

*Henderson Home News* publisher Moritz "Morry" Zenoff founded KBMI. Unlike Las Vegas stations that called Strip hotels home, the studios in Henderson occupied a converted two-bedroom bungalow built during World War II to house plant workers. Zenoff operated the station for two years before selling it to Television Company of America, which was in the process of launching a new television station on channel 13 in Las Vegas, KSHO.

KTOO also began in humble surroundings, frequently moving from locations that ranged from storefronts to a bug-infested trailer in the Ballerina Mobile Home Park, according to former employee Tom Willett. Original owners Thompson Magowan, Frederick V. Jones, and James W. Harford selected the call letters K-TOO based on the Reno station they owned, K-ONE. KTOO was the first 5,000-watt station licensed to the Las Vegas area; even though it bragged of being "Southern Nevada's most powerful radio station," it was only licensed to broadcast during daytime hours (from sunrise to sunset). According to FCC history cards, the call letters changed to KVOV in 1970 as the station adopted an urban format with studios in a former veterinary office on Boulder Highway and Sunset Road.

KBMI faced difficult times in the late 1950s; in the 1960s, they took on ratings powerhouse KENO with Top 40 programming. The station's most memorable DJ was Herman Schmerdley, also known as Tom Willett, who had also worked at KTOO. Broadcast Associates took over in 1972 and created the "Beautiful Music Island" on the station that was successful, according to manager Len Howard. Later in the decade, the station became all news before enjoying its biggest success as a country station. With the call letters KVEG, it changed frequency to 1410 and its city of license to North Las Vegas with power of 5,000 watts.

(A note about this chapter's title: "In Henderson, of course," is a line familiar to longtime Las Vegans—this was how Ben Stepman closed out commercials for his car dealership.)

March 11, 1954, marked the sign-on of Henderson's first radio station, KBMI, owned by Moritz "Morry" Zenoff, publisher of the *Henderson Home News*. In this photograph, chief engineer Mel North watches over on-air personality Vincent Brascia, who is sitting at the console. The station played the current hits of the day from the Chordettes, Sarah Vaughan, Ed Ames, Nat King Cole, and others. Brascia later worked at KLUC and KENO in Las Vegas. (Courtesy of Clark County Museum.)

Herman Schmerdley, also known as Tom Willett, is shown taking the FCC-required transmitter readings in front of the station's original transmitter, a 250-watt Gates BC-250-GY. When this photograph was taken in 1967, operators were required to take transmitter readings every hour, with some stations requiring them every 30 minutes. (Courtesy of Tom Willett.)

The author became quite a fan of KBMI in 1967 because next to KENO, they were the only other place on the dial he could hear the music that he enjoyed—the current hits of the day. The success of Top 40 was heavily dependent on tight playlists, strict structure, and consistency. It was a well-planned formula for success, which could take away the creativity of the medium, making it more predictable and less entertaining. Jocks like Herman Schmerdley (also known as Tom Willett) made the format shine through his talent, personal input, and creativity. (Courtesy of Tom Willett.)

Tom Willett, as Herman Schmerdley, entertained the audience while playing the hits. He left Las Vegas for Hollywood and had a successful career in television and movies as both an extra and a featured star in the television series *Dear John*, starring Judd Hirsch. He is visible in the background as an extra in nearly 100 feature films and television shows. (Courtesy of Tom Willett.)

Sunday morning at 8:10 a.m. is a time that those who work in the business call "God Squad." Elder Trent is shown here running the board, which normally is handled by a station board operator, on Sunday, April 23, 1967. This was one of KTOO's more luxurious locations next to the Bank of Las Vegas branch at 154 Water Street. KTOO moved here after operating in a mobile home. Part of the station's slogan—"most powerful radio station"—is visible on the studio window facing Water Street. (Courtesy of UNLV Library.)

As shown on this promotional image, "Basic Magnesium, Inc.," became "Beautiful Music Island" on KBMI. Broadcast Associates, Inc., owned by Steve Gold, Louie Weiner, Hank Thornley, and others, purchased the station effective on August 27, 1972. Two years later, after the group purchased KRGN-FM 101.9, both stations moved to studios in the rear of 1555 E. Flamingo Road. Around 1975, KBMI flipped from "beautiful music" to news/talk to become the first station of that kind in the Las Vegas market. (Courtesy of Tom Hawley.)

■ **KVEG(AM) Henderson, Nev.—Seeks CP to change city of license to North Las Vegas; change freq. to 1410 khz; change power 5 kw; install DA-N; add new nighttime TL: 0.7 mi. SE of Las Vegas Blvd. and Richmar Ave.; Henderson (two site operation); install new type trans., day and night. Ann. Dec. 1.**

In 1980, the final upgrade was made to KBMI, which was then known as KVEG (these are the most popular call letters in the area and have been used by at least six different stations in the Las Vegas market). This involved building a new site for nighttime use only with a five-tower directional array on Gomer Road south of the airport and a change in city of license to North Las Vegas, which is the only way the station could increase from 1,000 to 5,000 watts. In the mid-1990s, the station moved back to 1400 and abandoned the Gomer Road site. (Courtesy of *Broadcasting Magazine*.)

On January 15, 1973, KBMI finally moved studios out of Henderson to a trailer in the parking lot of the Hacienda Hotel on the Strip. While the surroundings may have been less than luxurious, the listener would never know, instead hearing the legal ID that proclaimed, "Broadcasting from the Hacienda Hotel on the Strip, this is K-B-M-I Henderson." This picture is from the 1970s. (Courtesy of the Nevada State Museum.)

KRAM studios were located at the Flamingo Hotel through the 1950s, with the hotel allotting glassed-in quarters for studios and offices facing the Flamingo Patio beginning on October 2, 1949, according to the trade magazine *Broadcasting Daily*. Even though KRAM was widely promoted to occupy the Desert Inn, as the hotel was under construction, the station was lured to more luxurious surroundings when the FCC allowed it to broadcast 24 hours a day; previously, it was daytime only. KRAM was located at the site of the unfinished Desert Inn for about a year in 1949, occupying a standalone building in front of the property, but moved just south to the Flamingo; KLAS-AM ended up spending the 1950s in the new Desert Inn. (Courtesy of the Nevada State Museum.)

# *Five*

# THE 1970S AND FM

Starting in the 1970s, FM became the new up-and-coming leader in the ratings as more vehicles became equipped with FM tuners and, ultimately, FM stereo sound. Audiences enjoyed crystal-clear reception and superior fidelity, and FM never had to sign off at sunset (as some AM stations did).

The first FM station in the Las Vegas area—and the state—signed on in 1948 as KENO-FM. At 103.9 MHz and only 360 watts from a 150-foot tower next to the studios, it had limited range, which was not necessarily a problem in a city that was small in population and footprint at that time. This station had a very short life, as it went dark after Max Kelch sold it in 1955. With very few FM radios and a small population, it was too soon for the Las Vegas market to support it.

KORK launched the first of its many FM signals in 1962, with the advantage of a tall television tower on Boulder Highway on which the station could mount its antennas, which improves the coverage area. Instead of duplicating the programming of its sister AM station, KORK carried beautiful automated music to cut operating expenses.

Another means allowing the survival of an initially struggling medium was the leasing of various auxiliary services on FM subcarriers to transmit closed-circuit programming such as Muzak. Max Kelch founded Las Vegas's first Muzak service, Muzair, after he sold KENO, according to his business partner Bud Weil.

Some FM stations (including KLUC and KVEG) simulcast AM programming, primarily because the AMs had to sign off at sunset. In the 1970s, FM made major improvements in audience share that led to the high-fidelity format overtaking AM by the end of the decade. KENO-AM enjoyed a lofty perch on top of the ratings in the 1960s only to see that lead chipped away by competitor KLUC. KENO purchased an FM station at 92.3 in 1977 to better compete with KLUC, a combination AM/FM station. "K-92" KENO FM became the first AOR station in Las Vegas in an answer to KLUC that program director Dave Anthony described as "Rock 40."

KFMS-FM flipped formats to take on KENO-FM with its own AOR format; curiously, the same company, Burkhart-Abrams, consulted for both stations. KFMS had a "Superstars" format, while KENO-FM evolved to be more like the AM station with a format called "Silver Blue and Gold." That was relatively short-lived, as KFMS flipped to country at the end of 1980, and KENO-FM went back to rock as KOMP.

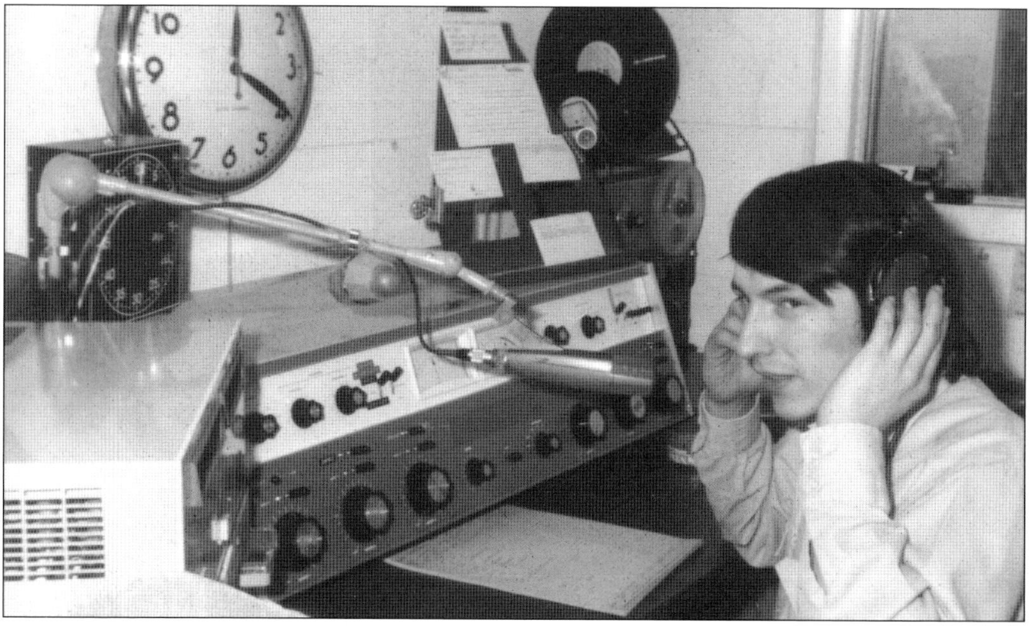

Keith Stewart is pictured in 1971 at the old KLUC studios at 3155 Industrial Road in the Industrial Arts Building. Even though the station's legal ID proclaimed "transmitting from the grounds of the fabulous Frontier Hotel," the studios only were on hotel grounds for the first few years, with the transmitter and tower on hotel property, which was right next to the studios across Industrial Road. Right below the station, on the first floor, was United Recording Studios, owned by Bill Porter, who was Elvis Presley's sound engineer. Porter did the final mix of Elvis's "Suspicious Minds" in this studio. (Courtesy of Keith Stewart.)

The Union Pacific main line ran directly behind the studios on Industrial Road. The on-air talent also served as newscasters who read a five-minute recap of the day's events at the top of every hour. No doubt, more than once, those newscasts featured the sound of a train in the background. Just below the station was United Recording Studios; producer Bones Howe called them "those infernal studios" in a *Billboard* magazine interview, because sessions had to be paused when trains passed by. Also, due to the close proximity of three radio station transmitters (KLUC, KENO, and KORK), interference would sneak in. (Courtesy of Keith Stewart.)

During the 1970s, KLUC took on KENO head-to-head with much the same playlists, but at night, KLUC became more progressive, playing hard rock after midnight on a show called "Spirit in the Dark" hosted by Bill Robbins. With the top-of-hour legal IDs voiced by Rod Serling of *Twilight Zone* fame, KLUC definitely had a more "hip" approach to classic 1970s FM, much like a skit done by Dan Ackroyd on *Saturday Night Live*. (Courtesy of Keith Stewart.)

Tom Robertson is pictured in the refurbished KLUC studios in 1971. Robertson moved into morning drive by the middle of the decade and became quite popular, as successful morning ratings helped drive ratings for the rest of the day. Jack Abell, Penrod Rideout, Jay Albright, Keith Stewart, and Bill Robbins handled other dayparts on "a most unusual radio station," as it was described in advertisements. (Courtesy of Keith Stewart.)

?LUC

98.5/F.M.STEREO 1140/A.M. VEGAS

TOP 40

Week Beginning October 6, 1971

| THIS WEEK | TITLE | ARTIST | LABEL | LAST WEEK |
|---|---|---|---|---|
| 1. | MAGGIE MAY | ROD STEWART | MERCURY | 1 |
| * 2. | The Night They Drove Dixie Down | Joan Baez | Vanguard | 2 |
| * 3. | Gypsys, Tramps, & Thieves | Cher | Kapp | 8 |
| * 4. | Superstar/Bless the Beasts | The Carpenters | A&M | 4 |
| * 5. | Uncle Albert/Too Many People | Paul & Linda McCartney | Apple | 3 |
| * 6. | Won't Get Fooled Again | The Who | Decca | 5 |
| * 7. | The Story in Your Eyes | The Moody Blues | Threshold | 7 |
| * 8. | Rain Dance | The Guess Who | RCA | 9 |
| * 9. | I've Found Someone of My Own | The Free Movement | Decca | 11 |
| *10. | Peace Train | Cat Stevens | A&M | 18 |
| *11. | Smackwater Jack | Carole King | Ode '70 | 12 |
| *12. | Sweet City Woman | The Stampeders | Bell | 14 |
| *13. | It's a Cryin' Shame | Gayle McCormick | Dunhill | 15 |
| *14. | If You Really Love Me | Stevie Wonder | Tamla | 16 |
| *15. | I Woke Up in Love This Morning | The Partridge Family | Bell | 13 |
| *16. | Spanish Harlem | Aretha Franklin | Atlantic | 6 |
| *17. | Theme from "Shaft" | Issac Hayes | Enterprise | 25 |
| *18. | Tired of Being Alone | Al Green | Hi | 20 |
| *19. | Birds of a Feather | The Raiders | Columbia | 19 |
| *20. | Only You Know and I Know | Delaney & Bonnie | Atco | 27 |
| 21. | Whatcha See is Whatcha Get | The Dramatics | Volt | 10 |
| *22. | Some of Shelly's Blues | The Nitty Gritty Dirt Band | United Art | 26 |
| 23. | Do You Know What I Mean | Lee Michaels | A&M | 22 |
| *24. | Imagine | John Lennon | Apple | -- |
| *25. | Spill the Wine | The Isley Brothers | T-Neck | 31 |
| *26. | Wild Night | Van Morrison | Warner Bros. | 35 |
| *27. | Hooked on a Thing Called Love | Denise LaSalle | Westbound | 32 |
| *28. | Smiling Faces Sometimes | The Undisputed Truth | Gordy | 17 |
| *29. | Valerie | Cymarron | Entrance | 30 |
| *30. | Ain't No Sunshine | Bill Withers | Sussex | 21 |
| *31. | Mother | Barbra Streisand | Columbia | -- |
| *32. | It's Only Love | Elvis Presley | RCA | -- |
| *33. | All My Trials | Ray Stevens | Barnaby | 29 |
| *34. | Where Evil Grows | The Poppy Family | London | 34 |
| *35. | What Are You Doing Sunday | Dawn | Bell | -- |
| *36. | Two Divided By Love | The Grass Roots | Dunhill | -- |
| 37. | Sapphire | Infinity | Uni | 38 |
| *38. | Respect Yourself | The Staples Singers | Stax | -- |
| *39. | Call My Name I'll Be There | Wilson Pickett | Atlantic | 39 |
| *40. | Ghetto Woman | B. B. King | ABC | 36 |

(*) Denotes Former Bonus Pick

BONUS PICKS: Everybody's Everything..........Santana................Columbia
Don't Wanna Live Inside Myself...Bee Gees...............Atco
Absolutely Right................5 Man Electrical Band...Lionel
Jennifer........................Bobby Sherman..........Metro Media
Gimme Some Lovin', Pt. 1 & 2.....Traffic, Etc...........United Art

The ?LUC Top Forty is based entirely upon listener requests, and this station's opinion of the record's audience appeal. It is not intended to reflect sales.

**JCPenney Record Department**

BOULEVARD MALL AND DOWNTOWN

**KLUC - The 24 Hour Music Festival**

Jack Abell 6 - 10 a.m. Jay Albright 10 - 2 p.m. Tom Robertson 2 - 6 p.m.
Keith Stewart 6 - Midnight Bill Robbins Midnight - 6 a.m.

WEEKENDS

Ron Dungee Dennis Hunt

The LUC Top 40 Week began on October 6, 1971. This was during the station's popular "find the missing 'K'" contest, in which Lady Luck has stolen the "K" in KLUC. Clues were given on the air as to where to find the missing letter, which launched listeners into a searching frenzy. The missing "K" was located thanks to help from the City of Las Vegas Street Department, which painted a sign with the message "Don't Walk on Red," which was mounted at the busy intersection of Las Vegas Boulevard South and Charleston Boulevard. (Courtesy of Keith Stewart.)

Pictured is a late-1970s black windbreaker sporting the KLUC logo of that era. This is in my wardrobe from my time spent working at the station from 1979 to 1982. By then, the station had its own studio building constructed specifically to house a radio station; the years of adapting to an office complex were behind it. (Courtesy of the author.)

My first paying gig was at automated Beautiful Music KLVM-94.1 FM. It was located in a two-bedroom World War II–era bungalow (like KBMI studios in the 1950s), and the radiation from the broadcast tower above the studios caused the fluorescent lights to glow even when they were turned off. Jim Flint was not only the station manager but also chief engineer. Later in the decade, Flint worked on the air as "The Old Professor" playing jazz and Big Band classics on KDWN radio; he was a mentor to me when I was an aspiring engineer. (Courtesy of the author.)

KFM Stereo 102

KFMS Radio
Las Vegas, Nevada
101.9 Mhz/20,000 watts (ERP)
Stereo/24 Hours

President and
General Manager: Steve Gold
Group Program Director: Doug Shane
KFMS Program Director: Jay Ford
KFMS Music Director: Keith Stewart

ALBUM ROCK COMES TO LAS VEGAS

In September, 1978...KFMS elected to drop its automated, Top-40 format in an all-out effort to fill the "rock vaccuum" in Las Vegas. In recent years, several stations here attempted so-called "album" formats...but most of these efforts fell short of truly satisfying today's rock & roll audience. The formats lacked excitement...the musical appeal was too broad to satisfy any one group...and, outside of rating periods, the stations were not promotion-oriented or doing much in the way of community involvement.

Only five weeks away from the Fall book, KFMS went "live" with a full-time air staff, under the consultation wing of the Burkhart-Abrams Superstars Network...and resulted in a 180 degree turn in trends for KFMS. And that momentum is still building our audience today as we continue to refine our airsound. We try to stay right on top of what our listeners really want to hear...through telephone requests, local record sales reports and "call-back" cards which give us input from the record buyers themselves.

KFMS air personalities are not your typical "hype" disc jockies...but rather come across as real people the audience can relate to. And they can be seen as well as heard. Whenever possible, the air staff gets involved with outside activities with and for our listening public. Good examples of this would be coverage of the recent Southern Nevada Youth Fair and the up-coming Kenny Roger's Celebrity Softball Match for charity.

Promotions are a vital part of the "winning rock" on KFMS. Examples:

WINDOW STICKER PROMOTION

...awarding various prizes to listeners for displaying a "102 Window Sticker" on their automobile. We are constantly spotting them on the streets giving winners everything from record albums to waterbeds to complete stereo systems.

ALADDIN THEATRE CONCERT PROMOTION

...offering 2 listeners a chance to see an upcoming concert free---complete with limousine service, dinner before the show, front-row seats, and meeting with the groups after the show.
And for those folks who can't make it to the concert, KFMS presents "THE NEXT BEST THING"...a re-creation of all the songs performed by the headline act...broadcast uninterrupted in concert sequence the night of the show.

THE KFM-102 ROAD RUNNER

...our station mascott! He's always out and about...cheering up people and helping the community in one way or another.

(more)

P.O. BOX 15223 LAS VEGAS, NEVADA 89114 TEL. (702) 732-7753

In September 1978, just over a year after competitor KENO-FM launched its album-rock format, KFM-102 executed its own take on the album-rock approach. KENO-FM had started to drift from an album-rock format to an album-pop approach, dropping many songs the program director deemed "too unfamiliar" and slowly steering the station in the same direction as KENO-AM. KFM was much more visible on the streets and emphasized personal appearances. There was an emphasis on community involvement. (Courtesy of Keith Stewart.)

Rick Diego and Keith Stewart both worked at KENO-FM. I also left KENO when I was offered the morning drive shift on KFM in 1979, replacing Doug Shane. Shane made me give him wake-up phone calls during my shift—not one or two, but at least five calls. Perhaps he was hoping I would turn that into a running bit on my show, but it only served to aggravate me. His critiques of my shows were quite brutal; now, years later, I realize he was bluntly trying to make me a better on-air talent. Ten years later, I worked for him again, but the second time around, he praised me and appreciated the help I gave him and the staff. (Both, courtesy of Keith Stewart.)

-2-

The 102 Road Runner was involved in the March of Dimes "Walk-a-Thon" this year...and also giving away turkeys last Thanksgiving. Just seeing the smiles light up people's faces makes this promotion worthwhile.

REGULAR MUSIC FEATURES:

"102 ALBUM HOUR"...Monday through Friday at Midnight
...tracking a major new release or a classic rock album.

"102 ALBUM FLIGHT"...Saturdays beginning at Midnight
...five classic rock albums tracked cover-to-cover.

COMMERCIAL FREE HALF HOURS
...30 minutes of non-stop music scheduled throughout the day.

MINI-CONCERTS...3 times a day
...3 songs back-to-back from the featured artist.

"AMERICAN TOP 40"...Saturdays, 8AM til Noon
...with host Casey Casem. The week's Top 40 best-selling singles.

"102 ALBUM COUNTDOWN"...Sundays, Noon til 3PM
...with KFMS Music Director Keith Stewart. The week's Top 30 best-selling rock albums for Las Vegas.

"102 SPECIAL OF THE WEEK"...Sundays, 9 til 10PM
...an hour of music & conversation with a major rock artist.

"KING BISCUIT FLOWER HOUR"...Sundays, 10 til 11PM
...major rock acts in concert.

SPECIAL MUSIC FEATURES:

"MINI CONCERT WEEKENDS"
3 songs back-to-back by each artist. A popular, often-repeated feature.

"BEATLES A-TO-Z"
Every Beatles song recorded in the studio...played back in alphabetical order!

"102 ALBUM POLL"
The Top 102 albums of all time for Las Vegas...tallied from listeners' votes.

"ALL REQUEST WEEKENDS"...and more!

PERSONALITY LINE-UP:

| | | |
|---|---|---|
| Mon. thru Fri. 6AM-10AM | DOUG SHANE | With 10 years of experience under his belt, Doug coordinates the efforts of all 6 stations in our broadcast group. His creative ability in the execution of hundreds of successful promotional campaigns is superceded only by his technical knowledge and production skill. |

-3-

| | | |
|---|---|---|
| Mon. thru Fri. 10AM-2PM Saturday, Noon to 6PM | JAY FORD | Before joining KFMS, Jay was Operations Manager at Z-93 and his management abilities really shine through his handling of the air staff and format execution as Program Director. Jay is also involved with agency commercials for radio and TV and has had good exposure throughout the media. |
| Mon. thru Fri. 2PM-7PM Sunday, 3PM to 9PM | RUSS RYAN | Russ got started in radio at Penn State University in 1972 as Program Director and morning man at their FM station. He's worked with many stations since, gathering top numbers in 18-49 demos. He comes across as a very personable guy...smooth & professional. |
| Mon. thru Fri. 7PM-12Mid. Saturdays, 6PM to 12Mid. | RICK DIEGO | A well-rounded background helps Rick do an excellent job in this important FM time slot. He's been an aide to a Texas State legislator, a sound engineer for a rock band, a cameraman for a TV station and Music Director for several radio stations...all this despite the fact he's the youngest member of the air staff. Rick knows his music and his audience...and they love to listen! |
| All-Nights | STEVE PIROSH | Steve is the newest addition to the 102 Air Force with 2 years of prior radio experience. He came to us from Lancaster, California and has attended the KIIS Radio Workshop. |
| Saturday, Sunday (Part-time) | BARRY FEHLER | |
| | TONY CARRISON | |
| | KEITH STEWART | As Music Director for KFMS, Keith spends 70 to 80% of his workweek devoted strictly to music...including a lot of listening to new releases, staying in contact with promotion people and planning many music specials for the station. He's had 9 years on-the-air experience in Las Vegas alone...having worked as Music Director for KLUC and KENO-FM in the past. |

Tom Willett (as Tom Kelley) is pictured in the KLAV-AM studios in 1978. Bob Broadbent was appointed receiver of the station after filing Chapter 11 bankruptcy a couple of years earlier. In 1962, the station also went bankrupt when Paul Schafer, the "Father of Automation," purchased the station (along with others) and installed his new automation system. He was trying to prove how a station could run without people, which failed when it was competing with live stations. The Gatesway board and reel-to-reels were leftovers from the automation era; a Seeburg record changer sat collecting dust at the transmitter site. (Courtesy of Tom Willett.)

I worked at KLAV from 1972 until 1977, the year before this picture was taken. New owner Alvin Korngold demoted me from program director when he took over but kept me on staff at the same salary—which some could view as a promotion in that my workload and headaches were lightened. Korngold fired our former engineer Gordon Atteberry, so for a brief period, I was in charge of keeping the station on the air. I built furniture as a sideline and constructed the cart shelves in the background; many more pieces of my artisanship are out of frame. (Courtesy of Tom Willett.)

KLAV owner Alvin Korngold managed to hire top-notch talent. Bill Carr worked mornings for a short time until being hired away by country station KRAM, according to Jim Duncan, country editor for *Radio & Records* magazine, in his May 12, 1978, column. On the KLAV station roster, Carr also was listed as music director. (Courtesy of Tom Hawley.)

One huge change for KLAV after Alvin Korngold took over was how contemporary it became. In the first part of the decade, the station targeted older adults with a safe—albeit boring—playlist featuring instrumentals and artists like Robert Goulet and Barbra Streisand. "Disco 123" arrived during the height of the disco craze and segued into "Superhit Radio" in 1979. (Courtesy of Tom Hawley.)

Pictured is the Superhit morning team: Jack London, Randy McGuire, and Floyd Thackrey. London worked at 50,000-watt KDWN. Thackrey graduated from Las Vegas High School in 1958 and was business manager of the school paper, the *Desert Breeze*. While in high school, he started his radio career as Jack Daniels at KRBO-AM; he worked at KENO-AM in the 1960s and at KDWN in the 1970s. Thackrey was in the Los Angeles, Phoenix, and Houston markets working with Top 40 programmer Bill Drake. Around the time of his passing in 2009, Thackrey was the publisher of the daily *TV Business Confidential*, headquartered in Milwaukee. (Courtesy of Tom Hawley.)

Pictured is KDWN's home. The studios initially overlooked a swimming pool that was atop the round porte cochere at the hotel entrance, and a domed restaurant shown in this photograph replaced it. KDWN did not have an easy path to signing on, facing stiff opposition from Chicago's WGN (also at 720), which objected, claiming interference from the new 50,000-watt signal. It took 11 years from the initial construction permit, issued in 1964, to the station's sign-on in 1975. One of the top directional array engineers in the business, Carl T. Jones, designed the transmitter plant; he was also a part-owner. KLUC also applied for a construction permit for the same power and frequency on that site; the FCC dismissed it. (Courtesy of the Nevada State Museum.)

For most of its early years, KVEG played country music, or "country and western," as it was branded. There was no shortage of talent on the station when this promotion ran, with Ted "TQ" Quillin in morning drive. I seem to recall the combo also drifting to pop music as well; "Marshall" Mike Davis was a jock I remember hearing on the station. Word has it that, according to those who have worked there, the studios were in a trailer in the parking lot. (Courtesy of Tom Hawley.)

After over 12 years of calling the Desert Inn home, in 1962, KLAS radio moved into temporary studios on the grounds of the Castaways Hotel (when it was the Sans Souci). The hotel closed that same year, no doubt prompting another move for the station to what Bob Stoldal described as the burned-out surroundings of El Rancho Vegas. The station bounced around a few more times before landing in Commercial Center, where it remained for around 15 years. (Courtesy of Allen Sandquist.)

# *Six*

# THE 1980S

Las Vegas was on its way to being the fastest-growing metro area in the country in 1980, as it was the third-fastest-growing market from 1980 to 1990 with a 60.1 percent growth rate, according to Brookings. The following decade, it was No. 1, with an astonishing 85.5 percent growth rate. This meant the market could support many more stations, and a slew of FMs signed on, including KUDO-93.1, KMZQ 100.5, KITT-96.3, KLVV 107.5 (which became KFBI), KRLV 106.5, KLSQ 95.5, KMMK 103.5, and KJUL 104.3.

Stations began to migrate from tower sites on the valley floor to antenna farms on Black Mountain Henderson and Arden along with Mount Potosi. All of these stations signed on with an adult contemporary (AC) format. After a couple of years, KITT changed its approach to classic rock. There were slight variations on the AC format, with some taking a soft approach; others, like KMMK, positioned stations with "Light and Bright Popular Favorites" so as to not appear to be "snooze music."

A major factor prompting the onslaught of AC was the tremendous ratings success of one station: KMZQ-FM, "Klassy 100." By the middle of the decade, KMZQ peaked with the fall book of 1986, achieving its highest ratings in history with 10.8 percent of 12-plus audience. The author's afternoon-drive air shift had the highest ratings for any AC daypart ever, with 12.4 percent of the audience, which was No. 1 of all stations. Being active in the community and responsive to what listeners wanted helped the station to achieve success. The MDA telethon, Easter Seals "Million Penny Drive," camping out at Las Vegas Harbor, broadcasting live to kick off the summer—these and many more promotions provided visibility and top-of-mind awareness. It also brought on heavy competition.

A few changes noted in the "comments" section of the fall 1986 ratings included that KORK/KYRK was sold by Donrey to Anchor for $3,250,000; KYYX changed calls to KLSQ and format from country to AC; and KUDO became the only station to leave the AC arena as it changed to KEYV and adopted a smooth jazz/new adult contemporary format. The market went from having two rock stations to having one rock station, with KFM flipping to country. In 1981, KENO-FM first positioned itself as "The Mob" and applied for the calls KMOB; after some objections (notably from Laura Belle Kelch, widow of Max Kelch), the station settled on KOMP.

This display ad for the then-new KUDO 93FM welcomed the 1981 NAB (National Association of Broadcasters) Convention to Las Vegas. This was the first station I recall as "mellow," which became a common take on the adult contemporary format. KUDO's studios were housed in the basement of the Barbary Coast hotel. The station was automated, with music played off reel-to-reel decks and commercials, liners, jingles, and station IDs played from a cart. Morning-drive shifts were hosted live, with the on-air talent manually starting and stopping the automation. (Courtesy of Tom Hawley.)

Around 1982, KUDO moved its studios to another basement, this time in the former Golf Club Hotel, which, by then, had become an annex of the Marina Hotel. The guest rooms directly above the studios would occasionally leak large quantities of water from overflowing bathtubs; the staff covered the water stains on the walls with music posters. This white furball appeared one day; apparently, she had been hiding in the old automation racks. She hung around and enjoyed the round-the-clock attention. The staff named her KUDO Kitty. (Photograph by the author.)

Finally, in the spring of 1984, KUDO moved across the parking lot to the top floor of the Tropicana Country Club. Originally, the top floor contained private bedrooms and bathrooms for special guests and a large banquet room. There were numerous secret passageways where one could often find a hotel employee hanging out on an extended break. The air-conditioning was woefully inadequate, as it was not designed to cool heat-generating radio equipment. There was also heat generated from the kitchens for the restaurant directly below the station; the smells were often good, but the heat was not. (Courtesy of the Nevada State Museum.)

Tim Maranville, also known as Randy Hart, was program director and hosted the morning show with sidekick Rodney Schumacher, a man of 1,000 voices. The characters in the artwork Maranville is holding portray the numerous characters Rodney played. Randy and Rodney wrote all their material, which was topical for their local audience. Randy Hart was the driving force responsible for the initial success of KUDO; later in the decade, he would achieve even better ratings at KMZQ "Klassy 100," as it enjoyed the best numbers in the station's history. (Courtesy of Tim Maranville.)

During the 1970s, KORK-FM was the clear ratings leader among the two "beautiful music" formatted stations—KORK and Henderson's KLVM. KLVM changed to sexier calls with KXTZ, and when John Parker purchased the station, the format was modified to feature live jocks during daytime hours. KORK-FM wanted to appear to make listeners feel good with a change to KEER, with the slogan "KLEER Makes You Feel Good," in 1983. (Courtesy of Tom Hawley.)

In 1984, The "Tuki Tuki Bird" roller skated into Las Vegas to herald an entirely different direction (and new call letters) for KORK along with a new slogan, "Let's Get Rockin'" with "Breakin' Rock" KYRK. "Power 97" soon took on market leader KLUC-FM. During its nine-year run, KYRK never did achieve its goal of beating KLUC, but along the way, it made for memorable radio with jocks like Anthony Miles. In 2003, the station flipped to the format it has today with new call letters: KXPT—97.1 The Point. (Courtesy of Tom Hawley.)

In August 1983, KMZQ-FM had a tight deadline to meet: it had to prepare to carry UNLV football games, as it had just been awarded the lucrative contract to be the host station to broadcast the games on the radio. The station succeeded, just barely, and signed on as "The Lite FM Q100." Jocks like Frankie Drew would often repeat this station positioning liner: "Q-100, where we never talk over the music." The production director was the legendary Jeff Colson. (Courtesy of Tom Hawley.)

Len Howard worked for Steve Gold at Broadcast Associates KFM/KVEG, but they parted ways in the early 1980s. Howard assembled the team who did radio play-by-play for the UNLV Rebels on KMZQ: (from left to right) Howard, Al Robbins, Randy Rosenbloom, and engineer Gordy Alsum. I worked with Alsum to build custom studio furniture at many of the stations around Las Vegas. (Courtesy of Len Howard.)

Klassy 100 was heavily involved in supporting charitable causes, with one of the biggest being the Jerry Lewis MDA Telethon. In 1986, the staff perched on a billboard at one of the city's busiest intersections, broadcasting live for 48 hours. Morning man/program director Randy Hart (a.k.a. Tim Maranville) remained on the billboard platform for the entire 48 hours. The station arranged for a couple of listeners to get married on the billboard, with the local CBS television affiliate showing the event live to promote the fundraiser. (Courtesy of the author.)

The North Las Vegas Fairshow, a weekend-long event benefitting the North Las Vegas Chamber of Commerce, was held annually and featured the largest hot-air balloon show in Nevada. Klassy 100 was the host station for the event from 1986 to 1991. As a promotion, four to five balloons prepared to launch over the Strip in October 1986. After taking off from the Landmark Hotel parking lot, I took my first hot-air balloon ride in the Landmark Balloon captained by Bob Smith. Equipped with a cellphone, I gave what were perhaps the first live airborne traffic reports on Las Vegas radio. (Courtesy of the author.)

Pictured is the Klassy 100 Living Room Suite at Cashman Field for the 1986 Jaycee State Fair. Ilene Diamond (left), Randy Hart (center), and George Thomas are shown doing Thomas's afternoon show live from the fair. If there was an event with an opportunity to meet and be involved with the public, Klassy 100 was there. Other events included those held on Memorial Day weekend, ushering in the summer while broadcasting live from Lake Mead Marina; the Hydroplane Races at Boulder Beach/Lake Mead; the Parade of Lights at Lake Mead; and the Easter Seals "Million Penny Drive." (Courtesy of the author.)

The staff called this the "Klassy 100 Microwave Van," because as a black-colored vehicle in the middle of the Mojave Desert, its surface and interior temperatures could get up to 140-plus degrees in the summer. That black paint job was very controversial. Originally, it was the "Pepsi Patrol Van," painted in Pepsi colors and adorned with the company's logos. Pepsi purchased the van for the station to use exclusively for "Pepsi Patrol" and associated prize giveaway events and was quite upset when it was repainted. This photograph, from the 1990 North Las Vegas Fairshow, was taken in front of the main stage. The person leaning on the front of the van is unidentified. (Courtesy of the author.)

This 1989 Las Vegas Jaycees State Fair flyer was used to promote "Jazz Night with Key-93." The former KUDO-93FM changed formats from adult contemporary to new adult contemporary/smooth jazz a couple of years earlier. Other events noted on this flyer include the KFM/7-Eleven "Date Nite" and K-News 970 sponsoring the "Moving Wall" exhibit that paid tribute to Vietnam veterans. (Courtesy of Tom Hawley.)

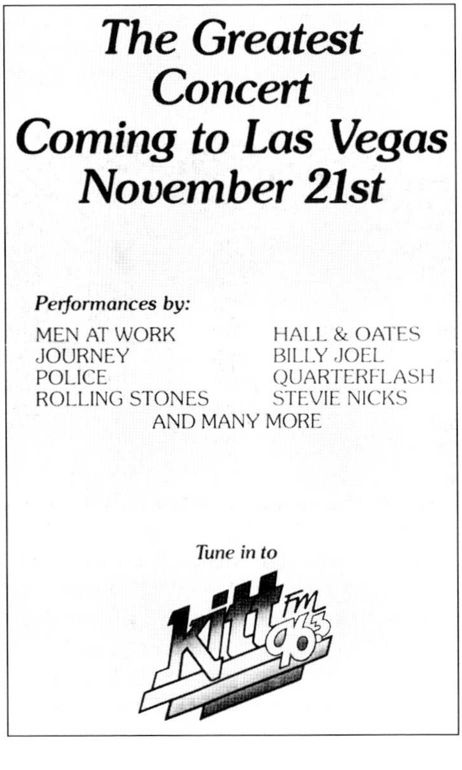


KRAM-AM finally got a sister FM station, although KITT 96.3 was not its first attempt. The July 25, 1960, issue of *Broadcasting Magazine* noted that KRAM's parent company applied for 100.5, duplicating its AM programming. It is not known why this never came to fruition, but in 1984, KITT signed on at 96.3. Dr. Donald Cole owned the two stations; when he sold them to "Seattle Phil" Sertall the following year, he handed each employee a crisp $100 bill. (Courtesy of Tom Hawley.)

Mount Potosi's first radio tenant moved on April 5, 1986—KLVV 107.5, an automated soft AC station. Dick Clark did television commercials for when the station segued to KUDA as "Oldies 108," and in 1993, the station embarked on its current direction with KFBI: "Howard Stern All Morning, Classic Rock All Day." In August 1996, American Radio Systems purchased the station, changing the calls to KXTE, Extreme Radio 107.5. The Extreme staff dressed up for Halloween 2003 at the cluster's annual costume party at Big Dog's; general managers Marty Basch and Tom Humm are chowing down in the distant background. (Photograph by the author.)

Art Kevin's KRRI was the mouse that roared. From its perch atop Red Mountain near Boulder City, it was the only Southern Nevada station that covered all of Lake Mead. Kevin moved to Vegas in 1982 after over 20 years in the Los Angeles market on KHJ and KMPC and founded the oldies station that same year. Art's son Ross, also known as Sam O'Neil, followed in his father's footsteps, first appearing on the air as "Rockin' Ross" and eventually starting his own production business, Word of Mouth Productions. O'Neil was the go-to guy for the "voice of God," and that voice was heard around the planet; he passed away from non-Hodgkin's lymphoma at age 40. (Courtesy of Tom Hawley.)

KORK-AM enjoyed success through the decades by being consistent in its format, always serving the higher-age demographic groups as a classic MOR station. In the 1980s, the station featured a nostalgia format—"50 years behind the times and proud of it." The personalities were all Las Vegas radio veterans, including Pete Moss from KRAM and KDWN and Jimmy Walker, who played Top 40 on KENO in the 1960s. In the previous decades, people tuned to Red McIlvaine, Walt Reno, Hal Morelli, Tru Hawkins, Chris Corey, and others. (Courtesy of Tom Hawley.)

# *Seven*

# The 1990s

This decade saw the entire broadcast industry change with the passage of the Telecommunications Act of 1996. Companies were no longer limited to owning 20 FM and 20 AM stations across the country and could now own up to 8 stations in a local market, which doubled—or in some cases, tripled—the number of stations that any given company could own.

Even before the passage of the Telecommunications Act, companies found ways to increase in size by taking over control of stations through LMA (local marketing agreements) and variations of it. Broadcast Associates was one of the first to enter this arena in Las Vegas with a joint sales agreement allowing the company to program KEYV, "The Key," flipping the format to "Hit Kickin' Country Y-93."

After the deregulation in 1996, the big fish began consuming the smaller fish. Regent Broadcasting purchased KFMS and KEYV along with KSNE 106.5. After adding KWNR 95.5 to the combo, Regent was consumed by Jacor, which was named after founder Terry Jacobs, who was CEO of Regent. American Radio Systems consumed KLUC 98.5, KMXB 94.1, KMZQ 100.5, KXTZ 107.5, and KXNT 840 AM; American Radio Systems was consumed by CBS Radio. Beasley Broadcasting later entered the feeding frenzy and consumed KKLZ 96.3, KDWN 720 AM, KVGS 107.9, KCYE 102.7, and KOAS 105.7.

Las Vegas continued to be the fastest-growing metro area in the country through the decade and into the new millennium. Outlying areas like the Moapa Valley and locations in Arizona along the Colorado River saw 100,000-watt FM stations emerging to feed the rapidly rising number of people in Las Vegas. New formats entered the market, with the most popular being the Hot AC format.

In May 1996, country-formatted KEYV was slated to change to "Mix 93.1" after being purchased by Regent. A new automation system was installed with the format already in place on the hard drives. Two days before launch, the competition at KMXB found out about the change and switched to "Mix 94.1" ahead of KEYV, quickly abandoning the station's urban format as 94 Jamz. The author ordered an oldies library at KEYV to replace the "mix" titles, and in two days, "Big Oldies 93" launched. This was an all-hands success at implementing a radical format change in such a short time; imaging director/production director, the late Sam O'Neil, really shined in his efforts.

The staff of KEYV is pictured at the station's Client Holiday Appreciation Party held at the top of the Landmark Hotel in 1991. It was a long-standing tradition for stations to host holiday parties to treat the people associated with their major advertising accounts. The staff dressed up in rented tuxedos and were able to join in the holiday festivities. Pictured here are, from left to right: (first row, seated) Mike Biggins, Tom Mulso, Cheryl Wright, Rick Morris, Tim Maranville, and Ilene Diamond; (second row, standing) Rick Denton, an unidentified salesperson, Jackie Selby, Esther Quisenberry, Shane Roth, the author, an unidentified salesperson, the traffic manager (name not known), and Kathleen Boyle. (Courtesy of the author.)

The author is shown being interviewed during a local segment of the 1991 Jerry Lewis MDA Telethon in front of the phone banks for the show. Local CBS affiliate KLAS-TV anchor Paula Francis is holding the mic in front of the author (right), and next to them are two unidentified representatives from 7-Eleven. The fundraiser was a weekend-long broadcast held on the roof of a local 7-Eleven. (Courtesy of the author.)

The author (right) is pictured at a live remote broadcast at a classic car show in 1992. The person on the left is unidentified. This picture is a reminder of an era when on-air talent did everything for a remote broadcast: hanging banners, assembling canopies, rigging up remote broadcast transmitters (RPUs), and trying not to be a sweat-soaked mess in the desert's 110-degree heat when listeners arrive. (Courtesy of the author.)

The author, program director for KEYV-FM 93 "The Key," is shown throwing the ceremonial first pitch at Cashman Field for the Las Vegas Stars in 1991. At the time, the AAA affiliate was the closest Las Vegas came to having a major-league team, and the local club became great partners with local radio and television stations in sponsoring special nights. This was the "Key Sports Tote Bag Night," with a certain number of fans who arrived early enough receiving a Stars/Key tote bag. What is most interesting are the ads on the outfield wall; most are for businesses that are long-gone from Southern Nevada. (Courtesy of the author.)

The author is shown standing behind the control board with a special guest on Y-93 "Hit Kickin' Country" in 1992 during the station's last days of broadcasting from the former fourplex on Desert Inn Road and Maryland Parkway. The roof leaked every time it rained, prompting the staff to have plastic sheets on hand to protect the equipment. Overall, it was a rundown building in a rough part of town. Others on the staff reported that the building was haunted, which would explain the odd vibe of the place. (Courtesy of the author.)

Pictured is the empty on-air studio for KKJJ "Jack" FM around 1999. The format was designed to be totally free of live on-air talent, or "jockless." A Windows XP workstation (on the left) played the hits without the need for human intervention. At the time this picture was taken, the staff consisted of one person who created the music logs; today, in most situations, one person will handle multiple stations. Software allows this to be done anywhere in the world; using the internet, daily logs may be transferred, and voice tracks can be uploaded as needed. (Courtesy of the author.)

This station signed on in March 1989 as Soft AC KMMK; in 1991, it was purchased by record producer George Tobin, who discovered pop artist Tiffany. His website states, "He owned and programmed KEDG FM radio 103.5, THE EDGE, in Las Vegas Nevada for 10 years picking all of the music the alternative station aired. In that period, the EDGE became *Billboard*'s radio station of the year and the highest-rated alternative in the United States." Tobin's son Dax, who was the general manager, was apparently more closely involved with the daily operation of the station. (Courtesy of Tom Hawley.)

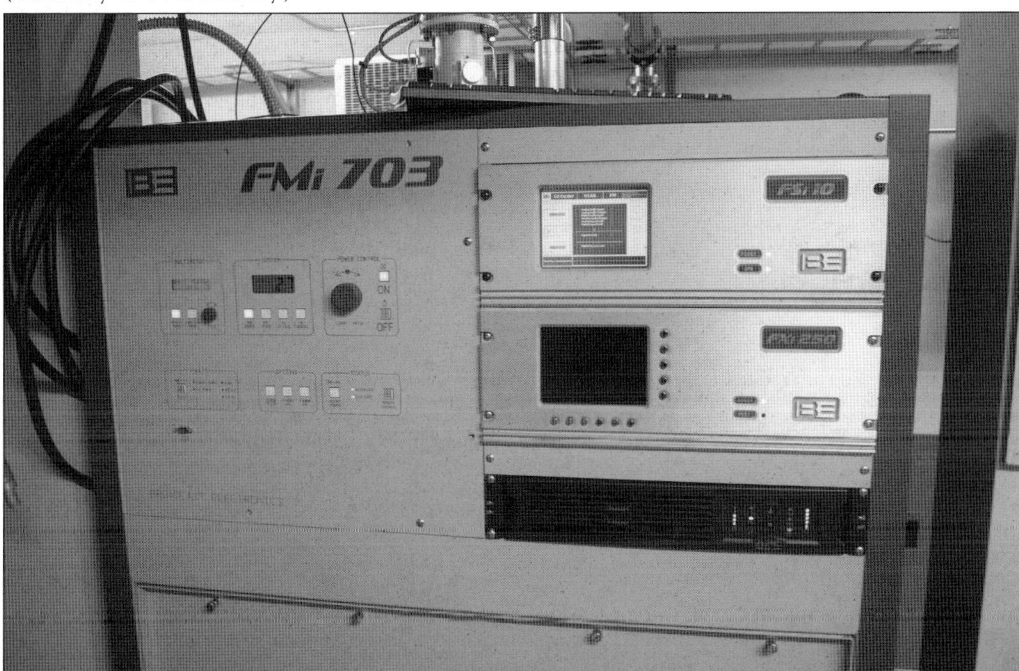


In the 1990s, computers became a major factor not only in studios but also at transmitter sites. Computer-controlled transmitting equipment began to evolve in this decade as it became more cost-effective as the technology matured. HD radio was in its infancy in the 1990s, with demonstrations at the NAB show in Las Vegas in the 1990s; in 2002, a standard was accepted. Pictured is an HD radio transmitter. (Photograph by the author.)

The author is pictured in the technical operations center (TOC) of a modern radio plant. This facility services seven stations—four AM and three FM. The most common gear includes industrial-strength computer servers. With new advances in audio distribution systems, audio over IP (AOIP) eliminates the need for a spaghetti-like mess of wires. Instead, a standard computer patch cable can handle a station's audio. Just as people stream Netflix into their living rooms, radio stations can stream audio to a receiver just about anywhere. (Courtesy of Howard Goldman.)

# *Eight*

# Television

Much like the city of Las Vegas, with its dazzling lights and big-name entertainers, the city's television history has likewise involved major showbiz figures and mysterious millionaires. There has been no shortage of controversy, with not one but two television stations losing their FCC licenses.

The key figure in the founding of Las Vegas's first television station, KLAS-TV, never played the showrooms in Vegas but was a larger-than-life personality who parlayed a $1,000 loan and an instinct for the mass media into fame, fortune, and perhaps the largest private land holdings in Southern Nevada: Herman M. Greenspun, who much preferred to be called "Hank." He drove from New York City to Las Vegas in 1947 to help a fledgling hotel get off the ground. The man who hired him as publicity director was Benjamin "Bugsy" Siegel.

Greenspun borrowed $1,000 to become part-owner of KRAM radio in 1950 but decided television was the medium, so he sold his radio station interest and filed for channel 8, with several furniture dealers interested in selling receivers in a state that, at the time, had no television stations. By 1955, he had acquired controlling interest as majority owner.

Through the 1950s, Greenspun, owner/publisher of the *Las Vegas Sun*, took on *Las Vegas Review-Journal* owner Don Reynolds as Reynolds launched the town's second television station, KLRJ-TV 2. Reynolds also filed a competing bid for Las Vegas's first cable television franchise, which Greenspun won. Reynolds was forced out of broadcasting in Las Vegas when the FCC refused to renew his license in 1976 because of "clipping" (inserting local commercials in place of network commercials and being paid to air both).

The third station in the area, KSHO TV-13, had suffered a similar fate. It struggled to be profitable a couple of years after signing on in May 1956 and operated under bankruptcy and in the red. The FCC refused KSHO's license renewal in August 1966—the first time the FCC had refused a contested license renewal.

Henderson was allotted a channel that became KHBV-TV 5; the "V" most likely stands for founder Charles Vanda, who was a patron of the arts. Channel 5 was not the first station in Henderson. KLRJ-TV 2 was actually first licensed in Henderson. Don Reynolds moved from the station's original facility in Henderson to Boulder Highway and Desert Inn Road. The FCC ultimately allowed the station to change its city of license to Las Vegas.

KLAS-TV's most intriguing owner, who bought the station so he could have it replay movies of his choice in the overnight hours, was Howard Hughes. He purchased channel 8 in 1968 to serve as his own personal Netflix and owned it until his death in 1976.

Targeted by Sen. Joe McCarthy for being a "commie" in 1960 and pardoned by Pres. John F. Kennedy, Herman M. Greenspun had been arrested and ultimately convicted of violating the US Neutrality Act by shipping weapons and ammunition to what would become the core of the Israel Defense Forces. He was fined $10,000 but served no prison time. Greenspun bought out R.G. Jolley's share of KLAS-TV to become majority owner and controller in 1957, but he never appeared on the KLAS radio ownership rosters. (Courtesy of UNLV Library.)

Hank Thornley brought his family to Las Vegas in 1962, when he became Nevada's first news director and television anchorman, creating the news department at KLAS-TV 8. He was elected city commissioner in 1969 and had an unsuccessful run for governor against Mike O'Callaghan. Thornley returned to broadcasting as news director and anchorman at KSHO-TV 13 and was part owner of Broadcast Associates with Steve Gold, Louie Wiener, and others. He lived to be 100 years old and passed away in 2018. (Courtesy of KLAS-TV.)

Technicians and engineers piled into the home of Desert Inn owner Wilbur Clark on May 15, 1957, for the filming of the popular CBS-TV show *Person to Person,* hosted by Edward R. Murrow. Murrow is the dean of American broadcast journalists and has won more awards than any other. The compartment doors on the sides of this camera were open to prevent overheating of the tubes—a common problem with this camera. In mid-May, temperatures in Las Vegas are typically around 105 degrees, and all that gear and people added to the heat load. (Courtesy of UNLV Library.)

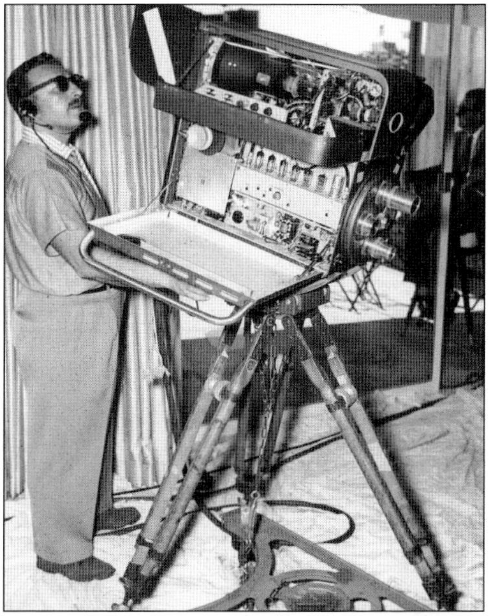

This unidentified engineer grimacing as he wrestles with a box labeled "DANGER" is probably unaware of the hidden danger involved; they were working in vegetation called oleander, which is poisonous. Oleander bushes were all over the Las Vegas Valley in the 1950s and 1960s because of their hardiness but were also prodigious producers of pollen. (Courtesy of UNLV Library.)

Technicians and engineers unload the CBS-TV trucks with gear to be used for the May 1957 recording of *Person to Person* at Wilbur and Toni Clark's home behind the Desert Inn at 331 E. Desert Inn Road. KLAS-TV did not have the proper gear for such an undertaking, so everything was trucked in from Los Angeles. (Courtesy of UNLV Library.)

CBS spared no expense in producing the popular *Person to Person* series. Host Edward R. Murrow first became a household name as a World War II war correspondent. Murrow's Wikipedia entry states: "A pioneer of radio and television news broadcasting, Murrow produced a series of reports on his television program *See It Now*, which helped lead to the censure of Senator Joseph McCarthy." Many people consider Murrow one of journalism's greatest figures—and the most well-paid. At his peak, he earned $300,000 per year, which was more than the network president made at the time. (Courtesy of UNLV Library.)

This is the November 9, 1971, Dunes Golf Tournament. From left to right are two unidentified men; Sen. Harry Reid; Joe Delaney, who wrote for the *Las Vegas Sun* and was a host on KRAM and KLAV; Forrest Duke, a *Las Vegas Review-Journal* columnist and host on KORK-AM; and Gus Giuffre, one of Las Vegas's most-beloved broadcasting personalities of the 1950s and 1960s. Giuffre is perhaps the only veteran of Las Vegas radio and television who has a street named after him. (Courtesy of UNLV Library.)

One can only imagine the headache brought on by setting up equipment that has traveled nearly 300 miles over less-than-ideal roads to Las Vegas. In 1957, the only route to Los Angeles was US Highway 91, which was then a two-lane highway. Almost all of the equipment was equipped with tubes, which have a habit of working loose from their sockets on a road trip. The engineers and technicians appear weary; there is quite an adjustment that must be made to endure the hot Vegas climate when one is accustomed to cool Southern California. (Courtesy of UNLV Library.)

On January 17, 1955, KLRJ became the Las Vegas Valley's second TV outlet, carrying both NBC and ABC networks. Three months before sign-on in October 1954, KLAS-TV requested a stay of an earlier grant by the FCC to allow channel 2 to locate its main studio outside of Henderson. An article in the October 11, 1954, issue of *Broadcasting Magazine* stated: "KLAS-TV filed an economic protest with the FCC charging the Henderson station's site is closer to Las Vegas, but KLRJ-TV has pointed out the cities are only eight miles apart and it always was known the ch. 2 station would serve both cities." The KLRJ studios and transmitter were on Boulder Highway, but in its advertising, it was called "Henderson Highway." On November 19, 1962, the call letters changed from KLRJ to KORK. Station owner Don Reynolds picked up the KORK calls when he bought the AM station in 1954. While KLRJ shows the affiliation with the *Las Vegas Review-Journal*, the KORK calls are more likely to be recalled by a viewer during the ratings process. (Both, courtesy of Tom Hawley.)

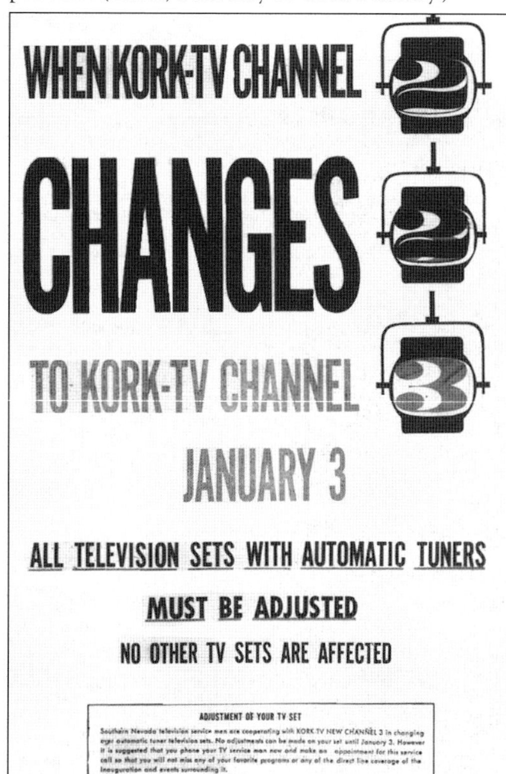

Pictured is Harold "Hal" Morelli, who was a city commissioner from 1971 to 1975. Morelli worked for KRAM in the 1950s and KORK radio in the 1960s before joining KORK-TV 2 as an afternoon movie host for a show called *2 on the Aisle*. The daily movie show was the filler between the noon soap operas and the after-school kids' shows like *Mickey Mouse Club*; channel 8 offered local content with *Hey Kids*, starring Dennis Hunt. Morelli had a successful run in politics as city commissioner. (Courtesy of UNLV Library.)

Channel 2 host Martin Black (far left) is pictured with Lionel Hampton (center) on Black's late-night TV show in 1960. While Hal Morelli and Gus Giuffre hosted movies during the afternoons, Black hosted a late-night movie, with guests appearing during the breaks, on *The Night Owl Club*. Other late-night fare was hosted by Milt Bozanik (*Vegas Days and Nights*) and Jack Kogan. (Courtesy of the Nevada State Museum.)

Without a doubt, the longest-running and most recognized sports director in Las Vegas television was KORK-TV's Dick Gregg. This advertisement from November 27, 1977, touts the 16-year veteran and eight-time award-winner as "Sportscaster of the Year." Gregg's friendly demeanor in his sportscasts matched his friendly nature; he attended all of the Little League ballgames to shoot footage and was very kind in person. (Courtesy of Tom Hawley.)

In a separate action last week, the review board added an issue against Valley to facilitate an investigation of the conduct of Meyer (Mike) Gold, a Valley vice president and 12.5% stockholder. Western had claimed that in requesting FCC permission in 1969 to sell KLUC-AM-FM Las Vegas, Mr. Gold had stated that the sale would permit him to devote more time to KLOM(AM) Lompoc, Calif., in which he holds a 50% interest. Despite this claim, Western had said, Mr. Gold now spends less time at KLOM than he did prior to the KLUC sale. While Mr. Gold had explained that he did not consider his presence at KLOM essential due to the competence his partner had shown in running that station, the review board found that inconsistencies between Mr. Gold's initial testimony and subsequent depositions could best be resolved in hearing.

The commission ruled that Western's and Valley's mutually exclusive applications for channel 3 in Las Vegas should be judged in a comparative hearing after merger plans that would have permitted the two firms to jointly operate KORK-TV fell through (BROADCASTING, Sept. 4). The merger was terminated after KORK-TV's renewal application was designated for hearing on clipping and fraudulent billing charges.

The March 26, 1973, issue of *Broadcasting Magazine* carried a story that did not bode well for the future of KORK and Don Reynolds's ownership. Las Vegas Valley Broadcasters challenged the license renewal of Western Broadcasting and Don Reynolds. Further complicating the renewal process, the FCC found KORK guilty of "double-dipping," in that they were charging clients for running network commercials but then were not running them. (Courtesy of *Broadcasting Magazine*.)

The headline in the July 11, 1974, issue of *Broadcasting Magazine* noted that "the baby goes with the bathwater" as both parties had their requests thrown out. The article states: "Even though the owner, Donald W. Reynolds Sr., was not involved in the day-to-day operation of the station, he should have exercised 'reasonable diligence' to prevent illegal 'clipping' network commercials instead of playing local spots while billing both network and local sponsors." (Courtesy of *Broadcasting Magazine*.)

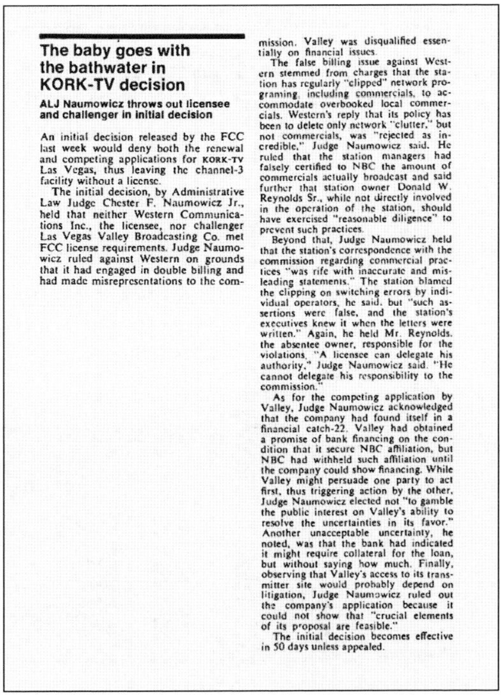

**The baby goes with the bathwater in KORK-TV decision**

**ALJ Naumowicz throws out licensee and challenger in initial decision**

An initial decision released by the FCC last week would deny both the renewal and competing applications for KORK-TV Las Vegas, thus leaving the channel-3 facility without a license.

The initial decision, by Administrative Law Judge Chester F. Naumowicz Jr., held that neither Western Communications Inc., the licensee, nor challenger Las Vegas Valley Broadcasting Co. met FCC license requirements. Judge Naumowicz ruled against Western on grounds that it had engaged in double billing and had made misrepresentations to the commission. Valley was disqualified essentially on financial issues.

The false billing issue against Western stemmed from charges that the station has regularly "clipped" network programing, including commercials, to accommodate overbooked local commercials. Western's reply that its policy has been to delete only network "clutter," but not commercials, was "rejected as incredible," Judge Naumowicz said. He ruled that the station managers had falsely certified to NBC the amount of commercials actually broadcast and said further that station owner Donald W. Reynolds Sr., while not directly involved in the operation of the station, should have exercised "reasonable diligence" to prevent such practices.

Beyond that, Judge Naumowicz held that the station's correspondence with the commission regarding commercial practices "was rife with inaccurate and misleading statements." The station blamed the clipping on switching errors by individual operators, he said, but "such assertions were false, and the station's executives knew it when the letters were written." Again, he held Mr. Reynolds, the absentee owner, responsible for the violations. "A licensee can delegate his authority," Judge Naumowicz said. "He cannot delegate his responsibility to the commission."

As for the competing application by Valley, Judge Naumowicz acknowledged that the company had found itself in a financial catch-22. Valley had obtained a promise of bank financing on the condition that it secure NBC affiliation, but NBC had withheld such affiliation until the company could show financing. While Valley might persuade one party to act first, thus triggering action by the other, Judge Naumowicz elected not "to gamble the public interest on Valley's ability to resolve the uncertainties in its favor." Another unacceptable uncertainty, he noted, was that the bank had indicated it might require collateral for the loan, but without saying how much. Finally, observing that Valley's access to its transmitter site would probably depend on litigation, Judge Naumowicz ruled out the company's application because it could not show that "crucial elements of its proposal are feasible."

The initial decision becomes effective in 50 days unless appealed.

On August 13, 1979, after nearly a decade of negotiations and back-and-forth in the courts, the new call letters indicated who won the license—"VBC" stood for Valley Broadcasting Company. Meyer "Mike" Gold was not part of the deal; instead, Jim Rogers took over, no doubt as an effort to appease the FCC. Rogers, a Las Vegas High School graduate, had local roots that appealed to the commission. (Courtesy of Tom Hawley.)

According to this advertisement, "KORK-TV-3's new news director Tom Siler knows that news is serious business," and he certainly looks the part of super-serious newsman. This may have been an answer to happy-time/good-news formats on other local stations, with consultants hired to offer suggestions to improve Nielsen ratings during newscasts. (Courtesy of Tom Hawley.)

No fancy-schmancy electric typewriter was necessary for "serious" news professional Tom Siler; the old Royal collecting dust in storage would do just fine. It appears that this picture was taken in the early 1970s, with fanfold teletype paper pinned to the walls. That feed-through, floor-mounted teletype machine clattered away at about 150 decibels and emitted an aroma similar to that of a lube bay at a gas station. (Courtesy of Tom Hawley.)

Channel 2 late-night host Martin Black (second from left) is pictured with Lionel Hampton (second from right) and a pair of unidentified go-go dancers in 1960. Live television was the norm in the late 1950s and early 1960s, before local stations had their own videotape machines. Black and other hosts often worked without cue cards and ad-libbed their shows. In the mid- to late 1960s, Black moved to channel 13 and hosted *The Night Owl Club*, where the live segments usually featured a paid sponsor, such as Herb from Nevada Blind and Floor. (Courtesy of the Nevada State Museum.)

• KSHO-TV Las Vegas, Nev.: 90% sold Mervyn L. Adelson, Irwin A. Molasky and Nathan Adelson to Nevada Broadcasters Fund Inc. for $137,000. Nevada Broadcasters principally owned by Reed R. Maxwell, 30%, and includes Joseph Bloom (Forjoe & Co. and Forjoe Tv Inc.), 5%; Howard D. Johnson (with interests in KNAN Salt Lake City, KSUB Cedar City and KVEL Vernal, all Utah; KBLI Blackfoot and KTLE Pocatello, both Idaho), 6.25%; James C. Wallentine (interests in KVEL Vernal and is buying KBRV Soda Springs, both Utah), 6.25%. Mervyn Adelson will retain 10% interest. President of Nevada Broadcasters, but owning no stock, is R.G. Jolley, owner of KLAS Las Vegas. Ch. 13 KSHO-TV is 11 kw affiliated with ABC.

KSHO-TV 13 was Las Vegas's third TV station, signing on May 4, 1956, under KBMI-AM owner Morry Zenoff. The following year, Zenoff sold it to Television Corporation of America. This October 26, 1959, article from Broadcasting Magazine features evidence of local owners with deep pockets selling their interest in Nevada Broadcasters Fund, Inc., the company that controlled KSHO-TV. Las Vegas residents will be familiar with the Nathan Adelson Hospice, which was founded by the successful businessperson who, along with his friend Irwin Molasky, built Sunrise Hospital. KLAS-AM radio owner and founder R.G. Jolley lent his media expertise to the venture. (Courtesy of *Broadcasting Magazine*.)

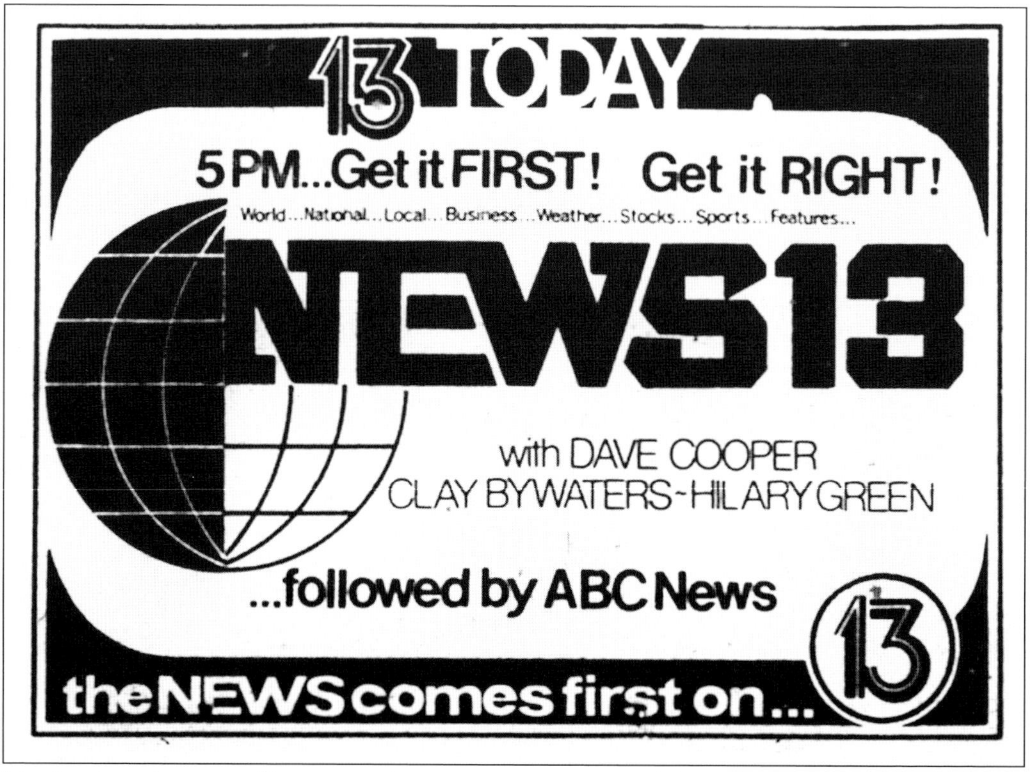


Heading into the new millennium, television stations promoted their news operations by changing branding and slogans, refraining from using the call letters and shifting to advertisements like the one shown here. "News 13, Where News Comes First" is now the only identifier for the stations. (Courtesy of Tom Hawley.)

First licensed on August 4, 1970, KHVB first set up shop at 1800 Boulder Highway in this building, which was originally a Flying A gas station. The quarters were quite cramped, which was definitely not what I expected when I went there in high school for a taping of *Young America Speaks* with Jack Kogan and saw that it was an old service station packed with television gear. (Photograph by the author.)

# Johnny Carson Group Buys TV-5

GORDON BASKIN
...LA Businessman

FORREST CHU
...Minority Leader

By KEN LANGBELL
SUN Staff Writer

A group including entertainer Johnny Carson has agreed to buy TV station KVVU Channel 5 for more than $5 million, KVVU President William Hernstadt said Monday.

Other members of the group include Las Vegas businessman Herb Kaufmann, Los Angeles businessman Gordon Baskin and a group headed by San Diego attorney Forrest Chu.

Chu told the SUN the other element included himself, another Asian-American and a Mexican-American.

Hernstadt cited as one of his reasons for selling a recent Federal Communications Commission (FCC) policy allowing tax deferrals to anyone selling a television station to members of a minority.

Kaufmann, asked why he decided to go into the television business, referred to the spectacular growth of Southern Nevada.

He became involved with Carson, he added, through mutual acquaintances. Also, he has worked with Carson on various charity events in Southern Nevada, such as United Way.

Hernstadt and his wife, Judith, own 94 percent of the stock in the present Nevada Independent Broadcasting Corp., which operates KVVU.

It has not been decided who will be president of what is tentatively being called the Johnny Carson Broadcasting Group, Kaufmann said.

Carson will have a top position, such as board chairman, and will play an active part in operating the station, Kaufmann said.

It is Carson's first venture into the owner-operator aspect of television. He rose to fame as host of the "Tonight Show" on NBC and is a Strip headliner.

Everything depends upon approval of the purchase by the FCC, Hernstadt emphasized. Until then, he said, he will operate KVVU on a "day-to-day" basis.

Hernstadt, meanwhile, is engaged in a legal battle, trying to obtain the license presently held by KORK-TV, an NBC affiliate which carries the Johnny Carson show.

The Donrey Media Group, owner of KORK-TV Channel 3, has been refused renewal of its license for several violations.

Hernstadt and another group, the Las Vegas Valley Broadcasting Co., have legal representation in Washington, D.C. trying to obtain the license.

At the same time, Donrey also is fighting to retain its license.

Speculation in the broadcasting business is rife that Hernstadt's sale and Carson's participation may somehow be

(Please See CARSON, Page 4)

TUESDAY
June 20, 1978
Las Vegas, Nevada
Vol. 28 No. 352

Las Vegas SUN

SUNrise Final
Late Sports

Southern Nevada's Only Home Owned Daily Newspaper   News 385-3111   64 PAGES   Circulation 382-3078

In 1978, TV-5 owner William Hernstadt announced the sale of the station to entertainer Johnny Carson in the Las Vegas Sun. It is not unusual for celebrity entertainers to own television and radio stations; Gene Autry amassed a large network of television and radio stations in major markets like Los Angeles and Phoenix. A group that included comedian Phyllis Diller competed for the KSHO-TV 13 license in May 1967 when its renewal was also denied. Hernstadt was in pursuit of a bigger fish—local NBC affiliate KORK-TV, which had its license renewal denied. Hernstadt lost his bid to get TV-3 to Las Vegas Valley Broadcasting, which became Valley Broadcasting. (Courtesy of Tom Hawley.)

# Donrey Media runs into double trouble with FCC

FCC has designated license-renewal application of one Donrey Media Group station for hearing, and notified second it is liable for $5,000 fine.

Commission ordered renewal hearing in case of KORK-TV Las Vegas on issues designed to determine whether station engaged in fraudulent billing practices or made misrepresentations to commission.

Notice of apparent liability sent to KFSA-TV Fort Smith, Ark., also involved allegation of fraudulent billing.

Question in each proceeding is whether station certified to network with which it is affiliated—NBC in case of KORK-TV, CBS in case of KFSA-TV—that it had broadcast network programs in their entirety, including commercials, when it had deleted some commercials and verified them as having been broadcast. KFSA-TV is also said to have engaged in double billing.

Misrepresentation issue in KORK-TV hearing order involves question of whether station was truthful concerning its policies or practices in joining network programs after they had begun, leaving before they had ended, or by extending network station or commercial breaks so as to affect network-program content.

Donrey may have additional problems in KORK-TV case. It had reached merger agreement with Las Vegas Valley Broadcasting Co. that was intended to end Valley's effort to displace KORK-TV's licensee, Western Communications Inc. But commission said it would defer consideration of agreement, under which Valley would get 50% of station.

It also said that if either party wants to terminate agreement, as it can under agreement's terms, and Valley decides to prosecute its application for KORK-TV's channel 3, subsequent order will be issued designating that application for hearing along with KORK-TV's renewal application.

Broadcasting Jun 12 1972
10

The 1970s were not good for Donrey Media Group and KORK. In 1971, Las Vegas Valley Broadcasting Co. challenged Donrey for the license renewal. Ultimately, the FCC refused to renew the station's license and awarded it to the challenger. Earlier in the decade, on March 6, 1972, fire destroyed the KORK studios on Boulder Highway. On March 13, after seven days of round-the-clock work and an amazing 4,363 hours of staff efforts, TV-3 again began broadcasting. On March 16, the UNLV Board of Regents granted the station permission to operate no later than August from the basement of the new humanities building on the UNLV campus. The station spent thousands on new equipment, and the agreement stipulated that the equipment remain behind after the station left. This was a win-win situation, with KORK able to get back on the air and UNLV gaining television studio equipment worth many thousands of dollars. After KORK left, UNLV communications classes were able to use a complete television studio. (Courtesy of *Broadcasting Magazine*.)

During the 1980s and 1990s, UHF stations popped up in the rapidly growing Las Vegas market, which eventually became one of the fastest-growing metropolitan areas in the country. While the market was rapidly changing, there was one thing that did not change: Mount Potosi problems. This roof failure in 2017 was caused by a heavy snow load and ice pieces falling off the towers above the building. Until the mid-1970s, all FM and TV stations used towers on the valley floor. KORK was the first to try to move a tower to Potosi; that was one reason that KORK changed to channel 3. Instead, it ended up on Black Mountain. KFMS-FM also sought a Potosi move and began constructing a cinder block building near the peak; the US Bureau of Land Management stopped that deal, since the station did not receive approval. (Courtesy of Tracy Teagarden.)

This is a recent view overlooking Las Vegas from Black Mountain, in Henderson, looking west. In 1969, when I became involved in the radio business, the Las Vegas metropolitan area was not even among the top 200 markets in the United States. As of 2020, it was the No. 31 market. (Courtesy of Tracy Teagarden.)

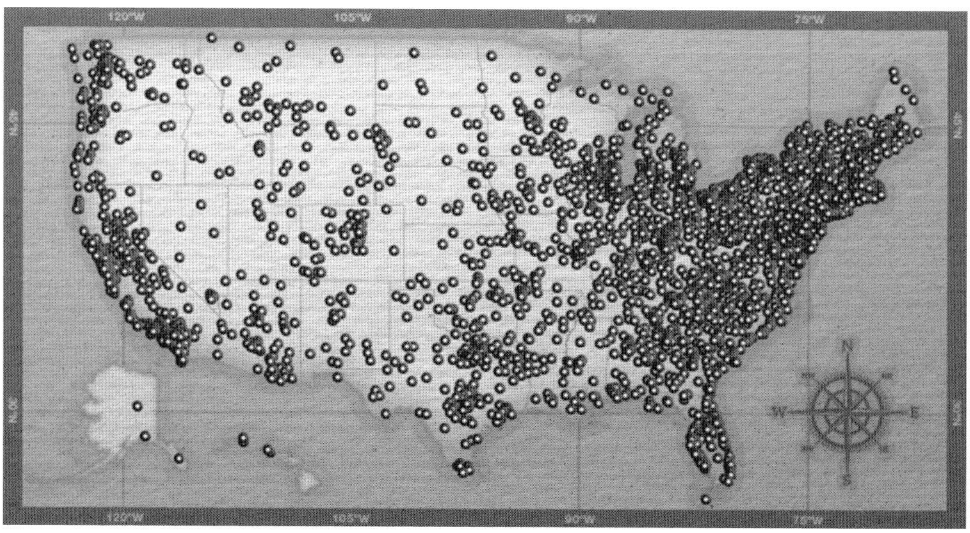



Consistent with our mission to preserve history on a local level, this book was printed in South Carolina on American-made paper and manufactured entirely in the United States. Products carrying the accredited Forest Stewardship Council (FSC) label are printed on 100 percent FSC-certified paper.

MADE IN THE USA